SCHRIFTENREIHE DES IMT 4

Schriftenreihe des Instituts für
Management und Tourismus

Herausgegeben von Christian Eilzer,
Bernd Eisenstein und Wolfgang Georg Arlt

T0344544

Wolfgang Georg Arlt (Ed.)

COTRI
Yearbook 2010

China's Outbound
Tourism Development.
Foreword by Taleb Rifai,
Secretary-General UNWTO

Martin Meidenbauer **»**

Dr. Wolfgang Georg Arlt, Studium der Sinologie,
Soziologie und Politologie an der FU Berlin (M.A.
und Dr. rer.pol.), Studienaufenthalte an der Fu-Jen
University Hsinchu/Taiwan und Chinese University
of Hong Kong. Reiseveranstalter, Organisator von
Messen und Ausstellungen, Consultant. Seit 2002
Professor für Tourismuswirtschaft, seit 2007
Studiengangsleiter International Tourism
Management an der FH Westküste.

Die Deutsche Bibliothek verzeichnet
diese Publikation in der Deutschen
Nationalbibliografie; detaillierte
bibliografische Daten sind im Internet
über http://dnb.ddb.de abrufbar.

© 2010 Martin Meidenbauer
Verlagsbuchhandlung, München

Printed in Germany

Gedruckt auf chlorfrei gebleichtem,
säurefreiem und alterungsbeständigem
Papier (ISO 9706)

ISBN 978-3-89975-191-8

Verlagsverzeichnis schickt gern:
Martin Meidenbauer Verlagsbuchhandlung
Erhardtstr. 8
D-80469 München

www.m-verlag.net

Index

Foreword

It is common knowledge that travel and tourism have become the world's largest and fastest growing industry. It is also an indisputable fact that tourism in Asia and the Pacific region is gradually changing the world tourism scenario because it has a proven record as the motor propelling global tourism. Within this global and regional tourism scope, I am pleased to underline the fact that China is firmly positioned at the head of the growth of Asia's tourism. China has surpassed all possible forecasts with the outstanding and constant growth of its tourism industry for more than a decade. It has consolidated its status as Asia's largest outbound tourism market, and at the same time it has shown a great potential as the most lucrative source market for tourism. Even at a time when the growth of international tourism has turned negative because of the global economic crisis, China's outbound tourism shows an increase in total numbers and therefore also an increase in importance for many destinations especially in Asia.

In addition to this, China is not only the most visited country of the Asian region and the fourth most popular destination of the world. It will also become the world's leading tourism destination by 2020 or even earlier, according to UNWTO forecasts.

This explosion in China's tourism growth has been more noticeable after its entry into the World Trade Organization in 2001, when Chinese tourists could visit only 18 destinations. However, to date China has granted to the majority of countries and regions in the world approved destination status for Chinese tourists. In 2001, 12.1 million Chinese travelled overseas. Last year, the number soared to 45.8 million.

The UNWTO has been maintaining close cooperation with China for many years. Through the existing bilateral and multi-lateral tourism cooperation mechanism, the Organization has supported important events such as the China-Japan-South Korea Ministerial Conference on Tourism, the Ministerial Conference on Tourism between China and ten ASEAN countries as well as promoting the tourism cooperation mechanism between China and EU nations. UNWTO has also been cooperating with China in expanding Pro-Poor Tourism, promoting the development of tourism destinations, making Hainan an international tourism island, and supporting the adoption of the Chinese language as one of the official languages of the Organization.

As the Secretary General of UNWTO, I am committed to supporting the work of China's tourism sector actively – a sector which is bound to play an ever-increasing role in the international tourism market.

I am thus pleased to see that the COTRI China Outbound Tourism Research Institute in Germany has been supporting the Chinese tourism industry. It has also been collaborating with the destinations receiving Chinese tourists through the dissemination of its research results, the organization of a number of workshops and other activities including the CTW Chinese Tourists Welcoming Award and the COQ China Outbound Tourism Quality Label.

The COTRI Yearbook 2010 offers a variety of articles from distinguished scholars and tourism experts from China and other countries. Readers will gain new insights into the development of outbound tourism from China to countries as diverse as Belgium, Germany, Jamaica and Mexico. They will also find practical information about how to increase the level of service quality for the specific needs of Chinese travellers. Owing to the wealth of information it contains, I am confident that it will be of interest to many, as the Chinese outbound tourism simply cannot be ignored by any important player in the global tourism market.

Taleb Rifai
Secretary-General
World Tourism Organization (UNWTO)

China Outbound Tourism in 2008-2009: Situation analysis and future projections

Zhang Guangrui

A few words at the beginning

The year 2008 was a year full of anxiety, worry and panic for the whole world. The economy was very unstable and went into recession, this was imputed mainly to the global financial downturn elicited by the subprime mortgage crisis from the world's superpower — the United States — continuing to develop, spread and deteriorate. Development of tourism is the barometer of world's political and economic situations, not only reflecting the changes on people's travel decisions, but also affecting expectations of future trends. Furthermore, changes in these situations directly impact on the operation of tourism-related industries, which in turn will retroact on tourism activities as well. However, reflections of this global economic situation varied in different regions, therefore, tourist consumptions from different countries around the world may not be completely in line with the overall economic situation. The Chinese outbound tourism in 2008 exemplified this point; the number of Chinese people travelling abroad achieved a growth rate of nearly 12% while the global international tourism increase was no more than 2%. Of course, it is conceivable that, if the Chinese did not meet so many "big events" and "difficult occurrences" in 2008, the growth rate of the outbound travel of Chinese citizens would have been even higher.

1. International tourism development worldwide in 2008

Early in 2009, the United Nations World Tourism Organization (UN-WTO) released the preliminary analysis on the world's tourism development in 2008. All together the following statements can be used to describe it: declining annual growth rate, worsened regional development, and worrying future. The number of international tourist arrivals worldwide reached 924 million, representing a 2% increase of 16 million compared to the year 2007. A temporal analysis indicated 5% growth for the

9

first half of the year but only 1% for the latter half. Tourism industry performed much better than the other industries like the real estate and car manufacturing, though it could not escape from the economic recession. The Asia-Pacific region, being the fastest-growing market in the world's international tourism in recent years, witnessed a colossal reduction in 2008, the growth rate slumped to 1.6% from 10.5% in 2007. Long-term promising Northeast Asia even registered a near zero growth which had not occurred in a very long time. Since 2000, on very rare occasions (for instance the SARS epidemic in 2003), the annual tourism growth rate in Northeast Asia had been 2-5% higher than the average growth rate in the Asia-Pacific region which was 50-100% higher than that of the world average. Notwithstanding, analysing from the number of international tourist arrivals, the ternary complex structure of "Europe–Asia–America" remained constant, in which the regions accounted for 53%, 20% and 16% respectively.[1] Table 1 below gives a thorough overview of worldwide tourism development over 2000-2008.

Year	The world's annual growth rate of international tourism (%)		The annual growth rate of international tourism in Asia-Pacific region (%)	
	Number of traveller	Tourism income	Number of traveller	Tourism income
2000	7.4	3.68	12.0	7.25
2001	0.0	-2.43	4.7	2.99
2002	2.9	3.89	7.9	9.15
2003	-1.7	9.50	-9.3	-2.96
2004	10.1	18.72	27.3	31.61
2005	5.5	7.56	7.8	8.73
2006	5.6	4.5	7.7	11.1
2007	6.9	5.6	10.5	11.4
2008	1.8		1.6	

Fig. 1: Comparison of global tourism growth rate against Asia-Pacific region 2000-2008[2]

---

[1] UNWTO World Tourism Barometer, January 2009.

[2] Data of 2000-2005 own calculation based on Tourism Market Trends, 2006 Edition, UNWTO; data of 2006-2007 from Tourism Highlights 2008, UNWTO; and data in 2008 from World Tourism Barometer UNTWO 2009.

2. Some new features on Chinese outbound tourism in 2008

Statistics released by the China National Tourism Administration (CNTA) showed mainland China in 2008 had in total 45,844,400 outbound departures, an 11.9% increase year-on-year, of which 40,131,200 were on private account and 5,713,200 on the others, progressing on the rates of 14.9% and 5.25% respectively. Ratio on these accounts was 87.5:12.5 while it was 85.3:14.7 in 2007. As shown in table 2, the ranking of top ten first-arrival outbound destinations of Chinese citizens didn't change much except for Thailand which dropped from the seventh to the ninth place with 13% less tourist arrivals, and Vietnam surpassing South Korea to the forth place welcoming a 58.5% more influx year-on-year.

Ranking (2008/2007)	First-arrival Destination	Number of Arrivals (in millions)	Annual Growth Rate (%)
1/1	Hong Kong SAR	17,557	8.80
2/2	Macau SAR	15,522	21.55
3/3	Japan	1,557	6.75
4/5	Vietnam	1,459	58.54
5/4	South Korea	1,374	4.71
6/6	Russia	0,790	7.12
7/8	USA	0,776	8.54
8/9	Singapore	0,713	10.04
9/7	Thailand	0,623	-13.15
10/10	Malaysia	0,623	8.56

Fig. 2: Top ten first-arrival outbound destinations of Chinese citizens and the growth rate of arrivals respectively in 2008[3]

2.1 While domestic tourism is restricted, outbound tourism is bound for psychological relaxation

The year 2008 was very special, many major events and natural catastrophes had significant impacts on domestic tourism such as the snowstorm

---

[3] Various National Tourism Administrations/Councils/Boards.

in South China at the beginning of the year, the devastating earthquake in May and the cancellation of the May Day Golden Week holidays, and finally the Olympic Games in Beijing. Therefore, in the second half of 2008, outbound tourism was very much vibrant particularly during the National Day holidays, Christmas and later the Spring Festival, albeit tourism price factors of the international market. One very important reason was that the accumulation of consumption demand on outbound tourism in the first half of 2008 and seeking for relaxation played a role in consumer decision-making process. Although at that time the world financial crisis had already stirred a lot of heated discussions, it seemed that the Chinese public did not really feel such a threat or precisely what they eyed on was the opportunity to travel.

2.2 Holiday adjustment activate the relatively condensed outbound tourism at the second half of the year

The adjustment for the Golden Week in 2008 had a significant impact on outbound travel, inducing a new phenomenon of a weak first half year and a condensed second half. The usual outbound tourism upsurge during the same time in previous years fell down because of the sudden cancellation of the May Day Golden Week, although the reasons varied, but one of which was both the tour operators and consumers failed to adjust and adapt to this change timely. Tour operators were not ready for short holiday products. Some simply gave up this opportunity and consumers felt that it was unrealistic to travel in short period of time and did not consider prolonging it by piecing together their other leaves in advance. A number of reasons, for instance lacking of suitable longer holidays in the first half 2008, and disappearance of other distracting factors like the Olympics, propelled restoring the outbound tourism during the National Day holidays, Christmas and the Spring Festival.

2.3 Number of people visiting the Special Administrative Regions (SARs) of Hong Kong and Macao maintained its growth

In 2008 tourist arrivals from Mainland to Hong Kong reached 17,557,000, an 8.8% increase year after year, among which occurred relatively more on shopping and mainly during the National Day holidays and Christmas. One important reason was that the RMB exchange rate against the HK dollar continued being strong, thus prices in Hong Kong were attractive and competitive. Some new policies introduced by the central government also made travel to Hong Kong more convenient. By the end of last year there were 49 cities in Mainland which could carry out the "individual visit" to Hong Kong, particularly non-registered residents in Shenzhen could participate in "Tours to Hong Kong" locally, furthering the scope and number of departure to Hong Kong. Meantime, the World Tourism Organization stated Macau was one of the successes among few destinations in 2008, which related a lot with the Mainland China visitors to Macau, under the umbrella that global tourism growth rate slowed down. According to the data released by the Macau Government Tourist Office, in 2008 more than 30 million[4] people visited Macau, a leap of 11% compared to the number of 2007, from which the number of arrivals from Mainland China to Macau was 17.5 million, representing 17 % growth year after year, and accounting for 57% share of the total Macau market with 2% increase year-on-year. In addition, this result was achieved after the Central Government and the Macau government in 2008 had made some policy adjustments on travelling endorsement from Mainland China to Macau; therefore it widely showed the vitality of this market segment.

3. Main factors influencing Chinese Outbound Tourism in 2008

In the "devastatingly tragic and overwhelmingly joyful" year of 2008, China's outbound tourism maintained a relatively high rate of growth on many accounts, among which the most important was that the Government developed more stable tourism policies: fewer and fewer restrictions were set for outbound travel; the decision-making of outbound travel was more of a personal choice and travellers could consider the time, place and manner of the consumption on their own. This development was also due to active PR and marketing activities conducted by

---

[4] According to news released on Feb. 25 2009 from the Statistics and Census Service Macao SAR (DSEC), Macao has made some adjustments to the original statistical system; the original publication of 30.18 million tourists in 2008 was "adjusted" to 22,900,000. It is necessary to distinguish visitors and other non-local residents in the number of visitors announced by Macau in the future.

the world's leading destinations. In addition, some specific reasons could also be generalized for this year.

3.1 The Central Government's support of regional tourism to Hong Kong and Macau

Hong Kong and Macau were the first tourist destinations which the Central Government agreed to open up as "individual tour" destinations for Mainland Chinese citizens; this special arrangement has made Mainland residents visit the two Special Administrative Regions (SARs) very convenient. Over the years, regions which could conduct "individual tour" to the two SARs kept expanding and maintained a strong demand. The relatively stable travel order and product quality in Hong Kong and Macao as well as competitive price advantages greatly enhanced their attractiveness to the Mainland residents. As in 2008 the May Day "Golden Week" changed into a "short holiday" and due to the safety concerns over some foreign tourist destinations, Hong Kong and Macao became alternative tourism destinations for Chinese Mainland residents.

3.2 New policy on travelling to Taiwan region

Since entering the 21st century, the cross-strait relations had been unusually delicate; the process of opening up of travel to Taiwan was also blurred and unpredictable. However, in 2008 a number of substantial leaps were achieved: "three direct links" across Taiwan Straits progressed much more rapid and thorough, than people generally predicted. During the year, alternation of the ruling party in Taiwan had created conditions for a two-way flow of cross-strait tourism. On June 13, 2008 Chen Yunlin, Chairman of Association for Relations Across the Taiwan Straits (ARATS) and Chiang Pin-kung, Chairman of the Straits Exchange Foundation (AEF) signed in Beijing the Cross-Strait Agreement Between ARATS and AEF Concerning Mainland Tourists Travelling to Taiwan. On July 4, Shao Qiwei, head of the Chinese National Tourism Administration, on behalf of the Cross-Strait Tourism Exchange Association (CTEA) led the first group of 753 Mainland visitors to Taiwan; as being a hallmark event for the cross-strait tourism industries, it marked the prelude for Mainland residents travelling to Taiwan. On July 18, tourism from Mainland to Taiwan officially started, ever since then it became one of the major businesses for tourism offices and tour operators in Mainland China. In November, more than 340 tourism professionals from Taiwan participated in a tourism fair held in Shanghai, heating up once again tourism promotions to Taiwan, which matured being the most popular destination of the year, although the real vacation tourist groups were not seen in Taiwan until the latter part of the year. Thirteen provinces and cities were included Beijing, Tianjin, Liaoning, Shanghai, Jiangsu, Zhejiang, Fujian, Shandong, Hubei, Guangdong, Chongqing, Yunnan, and Shaanxi, in the first batch of opening up tourism to Taiwan region. [5] According to the survey conducted by the Travel Agent Association of Taiwan (TAAT) on Mainland tourists, until November 30, the island saw a total of 44,000 mainland tourist arrivals, among which Beijing, Guangdong and Fujian ranked as the first three source markets. Generally speaking, the tourism market from Mainland to Taiwan kept a decent start of development. [6]

3.3 The United States as a new tourism destination

The United States was another hot spot for Chinese Outbound tourism in 2008. Though the Memorandum of Understanding, in which both governments agreed the United States as a designated destination for Chinese citizens, was signed in October 2007, it was not until May 15, 2008 that the China National Tourism Administration (CNTA) and the U.S. Department of Commerce announced jointly that from June 17th the Chinese citizens could travel to the United States in group form. In the meantime it also regulated, that in the first phase of a 6- month implementation period, only nine provinces (municipalities) in China could organize tours to the US: namely, Beijing, Tianjin, Hebei, Hubei, Hunan, Shanghai, Jiangsu, Zhejiang and Guangdong. The first Chinese citizen tour group had in total more than 250 people who flew to the United States, led by the head of the China National Tourism Administration Shao Qiwei on June 17th from Beijing, Shanghai and Guangzhou respectively, unveiling the curtain of Chinese citizens' leisure travel to the US. In spite of many obstacles such as high price and strict tourist visa granting, market potential was immense. "Novelty" also makes travel to the United States heat up.

---

[5] 12 provinces and autonomous regions on Chinese mainland, including Hebei, Shanxi, Jilin, Heilongjiang, Anhui, Jiangxi, Henan, Hunan, Guangxi Zhuang Autonomous Region, Hainan, Sichuan and Guizhou, were included as the second batch of areas opening tourism from mainland to Taiwan.

[6] http://travel.21cn.com/news/express/2008/12/23/5658713.shtml.

3.4 RMB remained strong, citizens travelling outbound in pursuit of good value for money

At the beginning of Chinese outbound tourism, what most people firstly were concerned about was where they could go, and then chose a destination according to their financial capacity. Especially for the general public there was no clear purpose and will, therefore price became the first main criteria for them in selection of a tourist destination. Furthermore, a considerable number of people did not have any experience of going abroad, and had little awareness on exchange rates of RMB against the other foreign currencies, coupled with the fact that the RMB could not be freely convertible. Therefore, minor variations in the exchange rates had not really caused many concerns. However, after more than a decade of development, the criteria of choosing outbound tourism destinations for Chinese citizens begin to change: people begin to pay attention to travel experiences and are no longer satisfied with the experience of "been here, done that". As barriers on free trading of foreign currencies in domestic banks eased off, more and more people were aware of the significance of exchange rates in travelling overseas and in consumption and financing. Therefore, since 2007 affected by the world financial crisis, appreciation of the RMB was paid much attention to. China's outbound tourists, particularly those who had shopping purposes, were very concerned about fluctuation in exchange rates at the tourist destination countries and regions; travelling to a place where RMB was more valuable began to draw attention. This was a new change in the last two years for Chinese outbound tourism, and was also an important factor for the increase in tours to Hong Kong and Macao, and this factor is likely to continue to have influence.

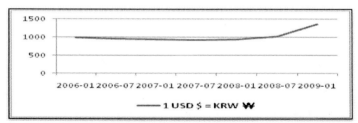

Fig. 3: Variation on exchange rate of one U.S. dollar against the South Korean Won from January 2006 to January 2009

Year	U.S. dollar	Euro	Japanese Yen	Hong Kong dollar
2000	827.97		7.9329	106.45
2001	827.68		7.0344	106.06
2002	827.67		6.2720	106.06
2003	827.70	878.22	7.0070	106.09
2004	827.68	1023.69	7.7656	106.54
2005	827.65	1077.83	8.0752	106.09
2006	806.48	974.83	6.9807	103.99
2007	779.54	1006.69	6.4900	99.945
2008	724.54	1077.57	6.7059	92.857
2009	683.92	901.71	7.6669	88.158

Fig. 4: Variation of Exchange Rate of major currencies to the RMB in 2000-2009 (every 100 foreign currency equivalent shown amount in Yuan)[7]

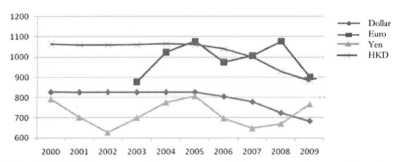

Fig. 5: Variation on exchange rate of four currencies against the RMB[8]

---

[7] "The conversion table of various currencies against the U.S. dollar" 1st issue annually, announced by the State Administration of Foreign Exchange.

[8] This figure is the diagram of the Table 3, showing the tendency of variation. Numbers shown on the left axis are not the value of a currency. Currencies shown: US$, Euro, Yen, HK$.

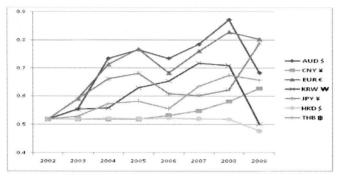

Fig. 6: Tendency of major currencies against the U.S. dollar[9]

3.5 Significant effect of publicity by various types of media

A very noteworthy phenomenon is that since the beginning of this century, the world shows universal attention on Chinese outbound tourism development: not only a growing number of countries have set up representative offices in China's capital and some important tourist generating cities, carrying out large-scale of promotion and marketing activities for the target markets, but also a proliferating account of foreign governmental tourism sectors and companies appear in a wide range of tourism expositions and fairs which target China's outbound tourism market, increasing the efforts of marketing and sales. While internet plays a vital role in tourism marketing, many overseas destinations have set up Chinese language websites specifically for the Chinese market, strengthening the supply of travel information. Another new phenomenon is that more and more magazines in China, with exquisite design, vivid pictures and coverage as well as with celebrity columns have increased the introduction of outbound tourist destinations, and have become very popular in China. It is a phenomenon not seen before, that such a large number of sophisticated print journals for its own citizens exist to promote the

---

[9] Description: This figure describes the variation on exchange rates of seven currencies against the U.S. dollar from 2002 to the beginning of 2009, not the value between each other. As could be seen from the figure, rise of the RMB remained stable; while the others elevated at first and then descended except Yen. Currencies shown: Patacas, RMB, Euro, Won, Yen, HK$, Bath.

overseas tourist destinations, and it is also uncommon in other countries. To some extent, this has propelled the desire of the Chinese to travel abroad, particularly the urban youth as the main potential tourists.

4. Some focuses on Chinese outbound tourism

4.1 Government strengthened the guidance of tourism to Taiwan

In June 2008, the Association for Relations Across the Taiwan Strait (ARATS) and the Straits Exchange Foundation (AEF) reached a consensus on issues such as cross-strait weekend charter flights and tourism to Taiwan, and soon implemented. The first ever leisure tour group from the Mainland to Taiwan departed on July 4; and on July 18, the tourism agreement on mainland residents travelling to Taiwan came into effect on both sides of the Strait, declaring a breakthrough in the one-way tourist flows across the Taiwan Strait. More gratifying to note is that on November 4, 2008, representatives from both sides of the Strait formally signed the documents such as the "Cross-strait Air Transport Agreement", the "Cross-strait Sea Transport Agreement" and the "Cross-strait Postal Service Agreement" and so on, declaring cross-strait direct air, shipping links and postal service long-awaited by the compatriots on both sides have become a reality.

On December 15, 2008 the direct air service (charter flights) was inaugurated officially. [10] It greatly reduced the flight time and distance, saved resources, reduced costs, and lowered the price of tour to Taiwan by

---

[10] According to the agreement, passenger charter flights, on the basis of the original weekend charter flights, increasing destinations and frequencies, are adjusted to normal flights. The Mainland side agrees on the basis of the original five destina tions of weekend charter flights as Beijing, Shanghai (Pudong), Guangzhou, Xiamen, Nanjing to open 16 more cities: Chengdu, Chongqing, Hangzhou, Dalian, Guilin, Shenzhen, Wuhan, Fuzhou, Qingdao, Changsha, Haikou, Kunming, Xi'an, Shenyang, Tianjin, Zhengzhou, as the passenger charter flights destinations. Taiwan agrees to open eight airports: Taipeh (CKS and SS), Kaohsiung, Taichung, Makung, Hualien, Kinmen, and Taitung as passenger char-ter flights destinations. In total, flights should not exceed 108 times in seven days and no more than 54 flights on either side. Flight frequencies will increase or de-crease depending on market demands.

around one thousand RMB. Naturally, this is a very good thing for tour operators and consumers.

Considering the reception capacity in Taiwan, the initial agreement sees a number of limitations on numbers of tourists, ways of grouping and prices. The result was not satisfactory. After the inauguration of direct flights, the Taiwan authorities have made some adjustments on the original conditions, such as, the tour must be in group form and no individual tourists; the size of tour groups must range from 10 to 40 people which can stay for less than 10 days. Revised requirement is that the size of the group is reduced to 5 people; and the length of stay is extended to 15 days. In addition, Taiwan also lowered the amount of security fund in the travel industry and the amount of withholding due to accident. The mainland side expanded the number of provinces that opened up tours to Taiwan from only 13 to 25, and more than 140 travel agencies were permitted to conduct businesses. In short, both Taiwan and the mainland are implementing the new policy seriously, and are also actively creating conditions to make cross-strait tourism more convenient and economic, despite early growth not being satisfactory. By the end of 2008, tourist number to Taiwan maintained around 10,000 people per month, though certain gap against the originally anticipated 3,000 departures on daily basis, however, this has been a pretty good start.

4.2 A particular incident changes the choice of destination

In August 2008, Beijing held the 29th Olympic Games; this was a hallmark event in China, it was also what the Chinese people anticipated for centuries. In order to pass the Olympic spirit on the others and showcase the achievements of China, in accordance with the international practices, the torch relay was organized in some countries. Terribly, for various political reasons, some western countries made irresponsible actions which hurt the feelings of the Chinese people, together with some unfair and discriminated treatments received by Chinese citizens while travelling abroad earlier of the year. It caused strong public dissatisfaction, with the result that before and after the Olympic Games part of citizens and travel agencies spontaneously boycotted tours to these countries and changed some of the original outbound travelling plans.

4.3 Non-legitimate "public sponsored trips" aroused government concern and public hatred

Pseudo "business trips and technical visits" are long-standing chronic illnesses. As Chinese outbound tourism continues to open up, there are a lot of changes in terms of the handling procedures and the means of travelling, so that some pseudo visits on public expense are often covered with a certain legitimate appearance. Exploiting policy loopholes has become a new form of corruption and embezzlement by the government officials and staff. In 2008 the media reported several typical cases which led to a lot of social repercussions.[11] According to incomplete statistics, from mid-May 2008 to the end of November the same year, China cancelled more than 1,100 approved and planned visits at public expense, with nearly 7,000 people; meanwhile, more than 550 pseudo visit groups with nearly 4,000 people in violation of the policies were suspended. To this end, the Central Government also specifically enforced actions to clear out outbound visitations at public expense, and it has made some effects: over the same period the number of holders with Passports for Public Affairs (Official Passports) who tried to go aboard declined 18.9%,[12] approximately 830,000 people less than previous year.

4.4 A new wave of border tourism

China has direct land borders with 15 countries. In the last century there were border tourism booms, which played an important role on the border region's economic and trade development. However, since entering the 21st century, especially after 2005 the neighbouring countries have established a large number of casinos to attract Chinese tourists, which have stemmed some serious acts of corruption and crime. The central and local governments took measures to stop the spread of this situation; as a result border tourism in some areas has been reduced or even stopped. Later on, in order to ensure the smooth organization of the Beijing Olympic Games, strict management and control was implemented on border tourism. At the same time, some of China's bordering

---

[11] Media in 2008 exposed typical cases in Zhaoqing, Guangdong province; Wenzhou, Zhejiang province; Xinyu, Jiangxi province; and Zhangjiagang, Jiangsu province, which caused widespread public hatred.
[12] "Beijing Youth Daily" on Jan. 6th 2009.

countries changed the original border entry and exit documents and procedures which the two sides used to agree to, thus complicating border tourism, and the original advantages were greatly reduced. There is no doubt that both Chinese and foreign tourism development in border areas and border trade have been greatly affected. Among bordering areas, for instance, Xinjiang Autonomous Region and Central Asian countries, southwest China and Vietnam, Laos as well as Northeast China and Russia and North Korea, all wish the governments to negotiate as soon as possible for interests of development on both sides, taking measures to reduce obstacles and expanding the exchange of two-way travels. There are reasons to believe that, under the impact of the global economic downturn and the frustrated development of long-haul international tourism, border tourism as an important form of international tourism may be even more prominent, and this type of outbound visits will once again gain attentions.

5.   Analysis of two issues in outbound tourism
Regarding the development of China's outbound tourism, there are two issues worthy of study, one is "Squeeze out the bubble" and "rectification", while the other one is "Setting up restriction" and "pave the way". The former is a statistical question; the latter is a policy issue.

5.1   "Squeezing out the bubble" and "rectification"
Since the 90's of the last century, China's outbound tourism has developed rapidly, which has drawn very much attention worldwide. China begins to be on the world stage of international tourism with the image of a major international great power in both tourism arrivals and departures. More and more foreign governments and tourism sectors not only are interested in "China Tourism" as a destination, but they pay great attention to "Chinese tourists" as a "star" of the market. Therefore, the international community has been focusing on the variations in policy statement on outbound tourism announced by the Chinese government, paying attention to the wording sequence of "three major tourism markets" and the use of adjective terms; in time, "ADS Agreement" and "Individual Travel Policy" of China have become buzzwords in describing outbound tourism. There is a special phenomenon, regarding China's tourism, the international community focuses the most on the facts and policies of the Chinese outbound sector, but in reality the amount of in-

formation in this regard is also the least, and the most difficult to obtain. In recent years, the Chinese state departments have regularly published figures on entry and exit of citizens annually, in which the main content is the number of inbound arrivals and outbound departures as well as subdivision of the travelling account, either on public or on private. Strictly speaking, this is not the outbound tourism statistics, only the records of entry and exit of citizens. It is flawless using them on measuring the extent of outbound tourism or studying consumption variations of outbound tourism. Here are two points of analysis.

5.1.1 Firstly, there are too many "bubbles" using this figure as the basis for tourism research.

Judging from the number of outbound Chinese departures released annually, it is not conducted in accordance with the UNWTO's statistical methodologies. As records of entry and exit, in strict sense, these are the (mere) registers of Chinese passport holders crossing the border, which include not only many tracking of "non overnight" with no statistical significance, but also those who do not fall into categorization of "tourist", as well as logging of those Chinese passport holders who do not reside in China. For example, the number of outbound tourism departures is 45,840,000 in 2008, among which 34,100,000 travelled to Hong Kong and Macao, accounting for 74% of the total. It is obvious that these measurements are inapt and have greatly exaggerated the actual size of China's outbound tourism. With a vague term of "number of departure" to determine the scale of outbound tourism is clearly a misleading, it is no wonder tourism officials from a number of European countries shouted, "being fooled on Chinese tourism statistics". The number of the outbound departures is a measurement of millions, rather than tens of millions; no to mention the ordinary people's leisure travel is definitely not the message from these official data. Therefore, relevant departments should carefully study statistical mechanism of China outbound tourism, and provide scientific date which reflects the (real situation), squeezing out the "bubbles".

5.1.2 Secondly, is the need to rectify the statistics of tourism between mainland and Hong Kong, Macao, Taiwan.

Due to historical reasons, before the return of Hong Kong and Macao to China, visitations to these two areas were often specially treated: non-domestic and non-foreign; but many policies classify them as "international" tourism. After the return and the establishment of Special Administrative Regions, the country resumes to exercise the power of sovereignty, but still there is a "border", as both sides differ on the political and economic systems, legal and currency matters and so on. Protocols which seem like "visa" and "Custom" need to be followed by crossing this "border", even though they are different from the (diplomatic) ones between countries. In the tourism statistics, terms like "outbound" and "inbound" are still applied to. It is clear that in more than a decade of time after the return of Hong Kong and Macao to the motherland, consideration should be given to adjust these tourism statistics series to reflect more about the concept of a big Chinese family. Similarly, after the mainland and Taiwan implemented the "three links", this statistical adjustment should also apply to Taiwan. A more suitable term should be given to these forms of travels, thus to "rectify".[13] Before becoming the "domestic tourism" officially, it should be at least separated from the "International Tourism", forming a single strand.

5.2 "Setting up restrictions" and "paving the way"

Over the years, China's outbound tourism has developed rapidly, so there were some concerns that the speed was too fast, and there should be restrictions, for instance, to collect departure tax like establishing a "gate". "Setting up restriction" is nothing more than "flow-regulation". In plain words, first it maybe because "too little water reserved then should not let it drain out"; or because "too much water may cause possible disaster on the lower reaches". If "water" in outbound travel referring to a nation's wealth, then, it appears that currently there is no need for the above-mentioned "closing" of the "gate", not to mention, such activities, as border crossings, are controlled by two "gates". If indeed "too much water may result in disaster", the destination countries and regions will naturally first make the decision of "setting up restriction". In the development of international tourism, the "gates" are often used; there are a variety of tools to control the "flow", at least, including administrative and economic means such as travel documents (passports and visas), number of quotas, means of entry and exit, foreign exchange

---

[13] Wang Xingbin from the Chinese Academy of Social Sciences Research Center, No.3, 2008.

control, taxation, etc. Indeed, some countries implemented or are still collecting "departure tax",[14] but the taxation has at least two different purposes: one is to restrict the number of departures, and the second is to raise money for tourism development. The former is usually temporary and will be lifted when the need to limit the number of outbound tourists does not exist anymore; while the latter is established mostly as means of raising money for tourism infrastructure or as the fund of tourism promotion. It might be reasonable if China sets up "gate" for the latter account, however, it will be irrational if it is set on the former reason. It should be noted that China's outbound tourism, till nowadays, is still in the long-term "gateway-based cost-cutting" phase, and the "gate" just opens a crack and many obvious limitations abounds. It is not necessary to re-tighten it. The things that need to do the most now are to "build bridges and pave the way" for Chinese outbound tourism, so that people can travel more freely, conveniently, safely and happily. China should leverage (foreign entities) to reduce barriers on visa application and means of transportation, etc., so that Chinese tourists are no longer subjected to disturbances, obstructions and unfair treatments such as discrimination, especially at the time when tourists use their own income to travel overseas. An unavoidable problem is that there is still a considerable distance at present for Chinese citizens to enjoy treatments, for instance, visa-waiver programmes and "individual travel". It is interesting to notice that in "Tourism Competitiveness Report in 2009" released by the World Economic Forum (WEF), there are two lowest rankings on the competitiveness of China's tourism (ranking 128 out of 133 countries), one of which is "visa" (that is, visitors to China must hold visa or countries enjoying visa-waiver treaty are less[15]), from another point of

---

[14] It should be noted that there are varied forms of "Departure tax", among which the "airport tax" is the most common. Usage of this tax is different; some are for airport infrastructures, some for airport security equipments and human resource costs, while some as a compensation for environmental pollution with air travel. Tourists are required to pay such cost, regardless of nationality; and they are invisible as they are directly included in the ticket price. Tax specifically on the outbound travel from its own citizens is rare worldwide. In fact, charges like "departure tax" are a double-edged sword, it can both influent the activities of its own people and it will also affect the entry of foreigners, because their burden also increases.

[15] World Economic Forum: The Travel & Tourism Competitiveness Report 2009. In the report the same ranking was 120 out of 130 in 2008.

view, diplomatic relations are reciprocal, this also restates the fact that visa-waiver treatments given to the Chinese people by foreign countries are also scarce. It is true that changes on this situation need the efforts of both China and foreign countries; and this is also the direction that the Chinese Government should put effort in for its citizens.

As for some government officials exploit outbound tourism for personal visitation and gambling, this is not the inevitable result of the opening of outbound tourism rather than management loopholes in government systems and delinquency of government administration, and therefore one should not "give up eating for fear of choking".

6. New development of China's outbound tourism in 2009

The depressed world economy since 2008 continues to plague the world, even once active economists seems to have become very cautious, and they are not optimistic about the recovery of business and consumer confidence; at least the first half of 2009 has remained this recession trend. The United Nations World Tourism Organization (UNWTO)[16] states that: "it is worthwhile to notice, as long as the current situation is uncertain, then there would be a lot contradictory information - many of them are just exaggeration or unfounded", ongoing concern towards financial and the economic crisis will naturally damage both confidence in business and consumers". More attention is now focused on the deteriorating situation in the emerging star market including Russia, India, Brazil and even China. The World Tourism Organization made the following prediction for the trend of tourism development in 2009 based on gained experience of the past crises:

- Travel to destinations closer to home, including domestic travel, is expected to be favoured as against long-haul travel;
- Segments such as visiting friends and relatives (VFR), repeat visitors, as well as special interest and independent travellers, are expected to be more resilient;

---

[16] More details from UNWTO: *World Tourism Barometer*, No.1, 2009.

- The decline in average length of stay, as well as expenditure, is projected to be more pronounced than the decline in overall volume;
- Destinations offering value for money and with favourable exchange rates have an advantage as price becomes a key issue;
- Late booking is expected to increase as uncertainty leads consumers to delay decision making and wait for special offers;
- Companies will and should concentrate on containment of costs in order to maintain their competitive edge.

It should be mentioned that these judgments stated by the World Tourism Organization based on experience are reasonable and worthy of attention. However, it is a general forecast. Some developments of China's outbound tourism in 2009 are the same like the world's general, but it is certain that, in many ways, they are different.

6.1 Importance attached on domestic tourism may impact on outbound tourism

Facing the impact of the deepening of world financial crisis on China, at present, the Central Government has formulated fundamental policies to "secure growth, expand domestic demand, and adjust the structure", and regarded the development of domestic tourism as an important area to stimulate domestic demand. To this end, the local governments have developed a series of policies and measures to promote local and domestic travels, which includes additional holiday(s), providing travel coupons, reducing price or exempting tickets to attractions. These measures are implemented not only in local areas, some even radiating to other localities, for instance, free tickets and coupons of attractions given by Beijing to the public in Tianjin; travel vouchers to Beijing residents by Hangzhou. These approaches are expected to expand further.[17] Even though the practical effects of these measures are still difficult to project, however, they will have certain impacts. Because these measures mainly pinpoint domestic tourism rather than outbound tourism, therefore, they might affect outbound tourism, though with minor penetration.

---

[17] Till the date that this article was finished, it was reported that provinces and cities like Hangzhou, Tianjin, Chongqing, Nanjing, Hunan, Zhenjiang, etc had given travel coupons to locals or other places visitors.

6.2 Travel abroad at public expense will be reduced and business travel will also be affected

Because of the catastrophes such as the earthquake in 2008, the State Council cut 5% of the governmental administration cost, which to a certain extent reduced the number and expenses of government staff going abroad. Meanwhile, through the special enforcement in 2008, protocols have become much more stringent and severe punishment will be imposed on any violation. In response to the 2009 economic recession, the State Council clearly states: "outbound tourism using public funds with various disguise is strictly prohibited," and explicitly regulated that "expenditures for official travel abroad must be compressed by 20% based on last three year's average with corresponding reduction on the number of departures".[18] At the same time, due to severe slump of export, business travel declined accordingly. It is foreseeable that this situation may also affect a wide range of non-self-financed trips such as MICE and incentive travels.

6.3 Trips to Hong Kong, Macao and Taiwan will be very popular with government supports

At the end of 2008, the Central Government put forward 14 economic measures in support of the Hong Kong Special Administrative Region, and expressed that these measures, in principle, also apply to the Macao SAR. It listed the support in construction of infrastructure, the deeper tripartite cooperation of Guangdong, Hong Kong and Macau, as well as new policies on Mainland residents travelling to SARs. It is believed that tourist arrivals to Hong Kong and Macao from Mainland in 2009 will increase substantially; in particular as this year is the tenth anniversary of Macao's return, series of celebration activities on both sides will generate new interests. 2008 was a breakthrough year for tourism across the Taiwan Strait; both understand that it was not easy. Therefore, everyone will value such a good time to do a good job. With the jurisdictional expansion of tours to Taiwan, growing numbers of tourism enterprises and more direct air routes and flights, not to mention Taiwan's efforts on optimizing tourism products and service quality, lowering prices, in 2009 there will be an exponential increase in the number of mainland tourists to Taiwan.

---

[18] "Beijing Youth Daily" Feb. 28, 2009.

6.4 Foreign tourist destinations have strengthened promotions to China

Because of economic crisis of the world economy, foreign countries and regions have high expectation about the source market of China. On one hand, promotions abound with more travel information and attractive prices. On the other hand, they would further simplify procedures for Chinese tourists on convenience. The Thai government has expressed a 4 months of visa-waiver policy, which is a signal; and the enlarged Schengen Agreement with more participating countries provides convenience for Chinese tourists with reduced cost. It is believed that these new policies and measures will play a role in the choice of the tourist destinations among Chinese travellers.

6.5 Safety concerns are addressed by Chinese tourists

For the whole world, 2008 was not a calm year: various disasters appeared now and then, including natural catastrophes beyond human capability to predict or to resist, as well as human tragedies such as terrorism, political turmoil, robbery and attacks. These all have affected international tourists including the Chinese. Therefore, on safety concerns, some Chinese tourists began paying more attention on destination choices; they have also raised the awareness of travel insurance as well as have set strict requirements on tour operators. Social conflicts will be more prominent in 2009 induced by bad economy, insufficient jobs and actual cut on incomes. The delicate and complex international relations will become more sensitive. To China this is undoubtedly also a severe test. Thus, the development of outbound tourism depends greatly on stabilities of home and abroad.

7. Concluding remarks

As for the concept of crisis, the Chinese have an unique interpretation and philosophy: "opportunity" abounds in "calamity". The economic crisis, being bad, is needed to be faced, to be dealt with. The whole world needs to seek opportunities. It may well be that 2009 is a new opportunity for China's Outbound Tourism, as more and more foreign destinations pay attention and meet the demands of Chinese tourists. It may well be that the market potential of China's outbound tourism has also become an important condition for cooperation between foreign countries and China. It may well be that the Chinese outbound tourism can leverage the favourable political and economic relations with destination countries and regions, uplifting China's national image and prestige in the world. 2009 sees rapid development of China's outbound tourism; it will also be the year in which many countries may make major policy adjustments on welcoming Chinese tourists.

References

China National Tourism Administration (2007, August 2008): *China Tourism Statistics Bulletin.*

UNWTO (2008): *Tourism Highlights.*

UNWTO (01. 2009): *World Tourism Barometer, No.1, Jan. World Economic Forum: The Travel & Tourism Competitiveness Report 2008.*

World Economic Forum (2009): *The Travel & Tourism Competitiveness Report 2009.*

Integration of China's Outbound Tourism into the Development of the People's Republic of China 1995-2010

Wolfgang Georg Arlt

1. Introduction

In 2010, China's outbound tourism is recognized by almost everybody in the tourism sector as having "significant benefits for world tourism".[19] This chapter will look at the long way the tourism source market China has come in the last 15 years and especially focus on the – sometimes reluctant – integration of the desire of the Chinese people for international mobility into the framework of the Chinese society and the policies of the Chinese government.

The text will discuss some aspects of the role that international travel plays in China and within the global tourism system at the beginning of the second decade of the 21st century as well as the ways in which the Chinese government has developed policies to make use of the growing number of international travellers from China in foreign and domestic policies. In conclusion, challenges and possible trends for the new decade will be addressed.

The year 1995 is the first year for which reliable or at least consistent statistical data for tourism in China are available. Before that date the database for the statistics was very shaky, with estimates based on anecdotal information (Xu 1999, CNTA 2004). For outbound tourism the statistical range was changed in 1997 and projected backwards to 1995, resulting in an old figure of 4.5 million outbound travellers and a revised figure of 7.1 million outbound travellers for 1995 (Arlt 2006).

The year 1995 is a good starting year with regard to the general condition of Chinas position in the world. The turmoil following the end of the bipolar world dominated by the USA and the Soviet Union had subsided, the temporary freeze of Chinas relations with the western world following the events on Tiananmen Square in 1989 had ended, and the second phase of the "Reform and Opening" process kicked off with

---

[19] Taleb Rifai, Secretary-General UNWTO (Lipman 2009).

Deng Xiaopings "inspection tour" to South China in early 1992 was well under way.

Still, all economic indicators were rather insignificant compared to today's levels. In 1995, the GDP of China was below 600 billion US$, in 2009 this figure stood at 4,326 billion US$, representing 7% of the world economy. China was not yet the country with the biggest foreign exchange reserves, neither the No. 1 exporting country in the world nor the No. 1 polluter. The GDP per person in PPP terms in 1995 amounted to 1,500 US$ only, whereas it reached 6,550 US$ in 2009. However, the Gini coefficient signalling the level of inequality of wealth distribution rose in the same period from below 0.3 to 0.5, changing China into one of the countries in the world with the biggest gap between the rich minority and the poor majority of the population (Guthrie 2006; Henson 2008; World Bank 2010).

Finally, the year 1995 marks also the moment in history when the Chinese government had to make up its mind how to react to the global acceptance of the right of free border crossing travel for almost all countries in rest of the world. The main problem had shifted for citizens of the former Soviet Union and its satellites from being granted the right to leave one's own country to the right to enter a foreign county due to the visa regimes. Many aspects like the growing affluence of part of the urban population of China, the growing integration of China into the world economy, the start of internet and other IT developments making communication easier and cheaper, the growing inbound tourism into China, the re-strengthening of relations with overseas Chinese living outside China and the increase in the numbers of Chinese studying outside of China, all contributed to the growing pressure by the more influential and aspiring part of population to travel abroad.

This had been possible since 1984 just in the form of family visits to Hong Kong, Macao and some Southeast Asian countries and in the form of study or inspection groups using government or state-owned companies funds to visit the major trading partner countries – both forms in fact often utilized for thinly veiled leisure trips. For citizens living close to neighbouring countries, border trips acted as another valve to release some of the demand pressure, sometimes taking the form of barter tourism (Zhao 1994).

The by now ubiquitous Approved Destination System (ADS) was therefore introduced in 1995, when agreements were made with Hong

Kong, Macao, and the Southeast Asian countries of Thailand, Singapore, Malaysia and the Philippines which had been covered by the earlier arrangements. Australia and New Zealand followed a few years later as the first new ADS destinations.

2. The role of outbound travel from China within the global tourism system at the beginning of the second decade of the 21st century

International tourism suffered a rare setback in its quantitative development in 2009. From 920 million border crossings in 2008 the number declined by 4% to 880 million (UNWTO 2010). China, on the opposite, reported an increase of 3.6% to a total number of 47.5 million border crossings by Mainland Chinese citizens. To many, the Chinese tourism source market resembles an island of positive development amongst an ocean of negative growth figures (Arlt 2010a).

In 1995 the seven million Chinese crossing a border amounted to little more than one percent of the total number of 534 million international travellers of that year. With limited spending power and hindered by complicated bureaucratic procedures to obtain passports, visa and hard currency, they did not attract a lot of attention from the global tourism community.

In the three quinquenniums (five-year periods) starting in 1995, the total number of border crossings more than doubled each time. In the first quinquennium 1995-1999 about 40 million Chinese persons went beyond the customs controls. The first quinquennium of the new millennium saw a rise to 88 million, an increase of 117% and the second one a still more pronounced growth of 226% to 200 million. Of the altogether 328 million border crossing reported by the Chinese authorities for the whole period, more than 60% happened with the five years period of 2005-2009.

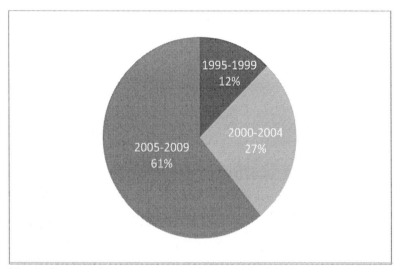

**Fig. 1: Share of Chinese outbound travels during three
quinquenniums 1995-2009[20]**

This does of course not mean that 310 million different persons or about one out of four Chinese travelled abroad. Frequent business travellers distort the picture as well as petty traders crossing the border almost every day to peddle their wares on the other side and especially regular day-trippers going from Guangdong to Hong Kong and Macao. Nevertheless with 200 million trips in the last quinquennium alone the overall number who had the chance to see some other part of the world has risen to a level unprecedented in Chinese history.

---

[20] Own calculation based on CNTA, COTRI.

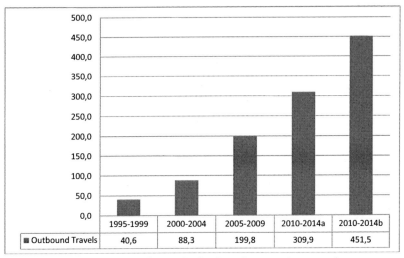

	1995-1999	2000-2004	2005-2009	2010-2014a	2010-2014b
▣ Outbound Travels	40,6	88,3	199,8	309,9	451,5

Fig. 2: Chinese outbound travels during three quinquenniums 1995-2009 in million border crossings[21]

On November 25th 2009, a State Council executive meeting chaired by Chinese Premier Wen Jiabao adopted the "Statement on Accelerating the Tourism Industry Development" which declared a planned annual increase of 9% for outbound tourism (Lipman 2009). If reality will follow the verdict of the State Council, this will translate into a considerable slowdown of outbound travels but will still add another 100 million border crossings to the total number of the third quinquennium of the 21st century. If however the growth rate of the previous quinquenniums would be reached again, the number would rise to a staggering 450 million border crossings.

Even the 47.5 million travels of 2009 put China already in a much different position compared to the year 1995. Chinese outbound tourism is an integrated part of international tourism responsible for 5.4% of all international travels. One out of 18 international travellers is starting his or her trip in Mainland China. China has been the major outbound tourism market in Asia for several years. With increases in the number of

---

[21] Own calculation based on CNTA, COTRI. a) Forecast according to State Council plan; b) forecast using growth rate 2005-2009 compared to 2000-2004.

Chinese travellers but decreases in the corresponding figures for Japan, it can be expected for 2010 that this prime position will be reached by China for the first time even if the visitors to Hong Kong and Macao are not included.

However, the number of travelling persons was not the only data that grew significantly. As a matter of fact, with 4% of the overall spending in international tourism in 2008, the share in terms of spending is still below the share in persons, but in absolute figures China has reached already the 5th position in the list of the world's major spenders in tourism after Germany, USA, UK and France, ahead of Italy and Japan. Translated into expenditure per capita on international tourism for the whole country, even with the rise from close to zero in 1995 and just 15 US$ at the beginning of the last quinquennium to 27 US$ in 2008, China is however still far below the global average of 140 US$ (UNWTO 2009).

3. Integration of Chinas outbound tourism into domestic policies

Before 1978, tourism (especially travelling for leisure) was considered by the Chinese government as a wasteful behaviour, as a sign of bourgeois lifestyle "which one should always guard against" (Zhang 1989) and as a potential source of unrest. That not only inbound tourism as an easy way to earn hard currency but also domestic tourism could play a major role in the economic development of China was very reluctantly acknowledged during the 1980s. "Domestic tourism policy was discussed and formulated at a time when much development had already taken place in many parts of the country" (Xu 1999: 75). In the 1990s domestic tourism started to be seen however as an important part of the service industry and an important element in the ideological switch from rural socialism to urban consumerism in China. Tourism today is seen as a "strategic pillar industry", which generated in 2009 close to two billion domestic tourism trips and close to a trillion Yuan RMB revenues (CNTA 2010), numbers which were planned by the Government to rise for 10% each year in the new decade (Lipman 2009), reaching an expected 3.3 billion domestic trips in 2020.

Outbound tourism had an even more difficult time to find acceptance with the Chinese government. From a dangerous activity bordering on treason to the "family visits" and "study tours" of the 1980s and 1990s, the doors were opened inch by inch. In 1995 the introduction of the ADS instrument and the announcement of the "Provisional Regulations on the Management of Outbound Travel by Chinese Citizens at Their Own Expense", which came into force in mid-1997 in parallel with the return of Hong Kong, seemed to guarantee a greater government control over the number and form of outbound travel and the amounts of hard currency spent. The chaotic growth years of the decade that followed demonstrated however clearly that the demand for international travel could not be contained so easily.

During an international tourism conference in 2007, Mr. Zhang Jian-zhong, Director of the Department of Policy and Regulation of China National Tourism Administration expressed a new attitude of the government policy describing it as "not encouraging and not restricting" outbound travel. He stated that on one hand, the government recognised the importance of outbound tourism in economic terms and in satisfying people's need, but on the other hand he still saw many aspects of outbound tourism that warranted „attention and further study", among them the question of individual travellers, religious travels, and the need to adjust outbound travel volumes according to inbound travel volumes. One year later, the same administrator already talked about further relaxations of control policies and measures, including the possibility of doing away with the control in outbound volume altogether (Tse 2009).

Other CNTA officials started in the same period to speak of tourism as being similar to a „Jue", an ancient bronze tripod vessel used for drinking wine in China 3,000 years ago, which could only be stand up if all three legs – inbound, domestic and outbound tourism – were properly and evenly developed.

To fight the global economic crisis, in 2009 the Chinese government on central and provincial levels issued a large number of vouchers which could be used for discounted travel within China and in some instances even for overseas travels. The already mentioned "Statement on Accelerating the Tourism Industry Development" of November 2009 finally sealed the official acknowledgement of outbound tourism as being on an equal footing with inbound and domestic tourism.

For the affluent Chinese consumers international travel has become especially in the last five years an integrated part of the set of conspicuous consumption together with the private car, the private gated-community apartment and branded goods. The red tape connected to crossing the border has been significantly reduced especially for the citizens of the big cities like Beijing, Shanghai and Guangzhou. Magazines, TV shows, marketing campaigns by National Tourism Organisations and Destination Marketing Organisations in pedestrian areas and shopping centers, stories by neighbours and colleagues, internet sources and movies all play their role in changing the idea of going abroad for leisure and status enhancement from a faint dream in 1995 to a realistic aspiration of a growing number of better-off citizens.

Leveraging political or economic influence to enjoy leisure outbound trips paid by government bodies or companies is still existing, despite the recurring, but normally short-lived campaigns against this malpractice (comp. Zhang in this book). However, with the increasing wealth of the upper levels of the Chinese society, the number of pseudo-business travels is decreasing.

Together with consumerism, nationalism or "patriotism" is another aspect of the new ideological set-up that superseded in many respects the former Maoist ontology in China (Arlt 2010b). China, "a civilization pretending to be a nation-state" (Pye 1996: 109) is using tourism as a tool to create a national identity (Palmer 1998) across the vast differences of the history, customs and languages of the different parts of today's China with the visits to cultural and natural sights connected to Chinese ancient history and culture. Since 2005 "Red tourism" is another form of promoting "patriotism and loyalty towards the Communist party". Several hundred million travellers have been joining subsidised tour groups visiting places and sights connected to the history of the Chinese revolution (Steinmetz 2007).

Travelling abroad is often discussed in China as a way of demonstrating the "soft power" of China. During a Tourism Forum in Hong Kong in 2007, Mr. Shao Qiwei, Chairman of China National Tourism Administration used this term in his keynote address.

"In the case of China, it is postulated that China could elevate its international status by sending abroad visitors with high spending power. China could command political superiority in being able to control the outflow of tourists to a particular country, and hence the tourism income in that country. China could also command political recognition and respect in being seen to be actively and openly promoting outbound tourism to the world, and through organising or sponsoring outbound travel trade and consumer shows." (Tse 2009: 257).

The motivation for many Chinese travellers to demonstrate to their peer groups inside China that they can afford international travel therefore is increasingly merged with the motivation to demonstrate to the outside world that the travellers as a Chinese is able to fritter away hard currency on leisure trips and shopping sprees outside China.

4. Integration of Chinas outbound tourism into foreign policies

The Approved Destination Status system was meant to control the flow of Chinese citizens to other countries and regions through bilateral agreements. In the first years after the introduction, ADS agreements were the result of long and protracted negotiations. Complicated rules of reciprocity and other limitations were included, with seven preconditions to be met by the applying country:

- The country should be a source market of outbound tourists to China.
- The country should have good political relationships with China.
- Tourism resources should be attractive and facilities suitable for Chinese travellers.
- Safety and freedom from discrimination for the Chinese travellers should be guaranteed.
- The country should be easily accessible from China.
- The expenditure of tourists from the country visiting China should be balanced with the expenditure of Chinese tourists travelling to that country.
- The number of tourists from the country and from China should only increase reciprocally.

These kinds of restrictions clearly were impossible to meet for most countries in the world, which could neither guarantee total safety nor force their own citizens to visit China and to spend a specific sum of money there.

With the rapid development of the Chinese outbound tourism, however, the speed of successful discussions increased. Many countries that were awarded ADS do not meet many of the seven limitations, being either no source market for tourism to China, or having no direct air link, or being short of Chinese restaurants and Chinese-speaking guides, or all of these.

Outbound tourism and ADS started also more and more to be used by the Chinese Government as a diplomatic tool. ADS was given as a kind of "gift" to countries that in terms of tourism business are insignificant (Arlt 2006).

Africa can be used as an example of the growing insight of the Chinese government that outbound tourism represents not only a drain of funds but an opportunity to create goodwill. Among the topics needing attention and further study mentioned by Zhang Jianzhong (CNTA) in 2007 could also be found the "Use of outbound tourism as a means to address trade balance" (Tse 2009). The Japanese government promoted outbound tourism to the USA in the 1970s and 1980s to show the willingness to decrease the American merchandise trade deficit of that time through tourism spending by Japanese tourists in the USA. The Chinese government has used this instrument with more effect in Africa.

Africa has been a part of the Chinese foreign policy within the system of the "Three Worlds". Support for African countries – the construction of the TanZam railway in the early 1970s being the most famous example – helped China to establish diplomatic relations and to win the seat for China in the UN assembly.

In 1996, the then President of China, Jiang Zemin, visited Africa, starting a period of relations based more on economic than on political common interests. For example, in 2004 Chinese Premier Wen Jiabao announced at the First China-Africa Cooperation Forum that the Chinese government would grant ADS to eight African countries. More countries followed during the second Forum on China-Africa Cooperation in November 2006, which gathered all 48 African heads of State of the countries having diplomatic relations with China in Beijing.

The Summit adopted a declaration proclaiming establishment of "a new type of strategic partnership" between China and Africa. It was agreed that China and Africa should fully tap cooperation potential and strive to bring their trade volume to 100 billion U.S. dollars by 2010 from about 40 billion U.S. dollars in 2005. In fact this goal was already reached in 2008 with a total trade volume between China and Africa of 107 billion US$ in 2008.

Beside trade, China is also the most important source for Foreign Direct Investment (FDI) in Sub-Saharan Africa. Almost 1,000 Chinese companies, most of them state-owned, have invested almost all African countries, mainly in the fields of natural resources extraction, infrastructure, telecommunication, agriculture and retail. This reflects the rapid development of Chinas outbound FDI which developed from insignificant levels in 2004 to 150 billion US$ in 2009, exceeding the flow of FDI into China and turning China for the first time into a capital exporter (Renmin Ribao 2009). About 100,000 Chinese workers are supposed to be working in Chinese-African joint ventures (Rosen, Hanemann 2009).

Within the overall strategy of Chinese government of developing closer economic ties with Africa, it is also strongly supporting Chinese outbound travel to Africa and encouraging Chinese to travel to Africa for business and leisure. During President Hu Jintao's visit to Africa in February 2009, already the second since the China-Africa Summit in 2006, the further improvement of tourism ties was named as one of the fields of strengthened future cooperation.

Most of the African countries have been given the opportunity to sign agreements with China for the establishment of the Approved Destination Status and the Chinese government has actively encouraged Chinese tourists to visit the continent, pointing to the fact that this can be seen as an indirect development aid for the African countries.

5. Challenges and Trends

Travelling and also travelling literature played an important role in the process of creation and development of the cultural identity of the Chinese already in Imperial times. Travel diaries (Youji) flourished from the Tang Dynasty (618-907) onwards and travelling was seen as a source of education as well as a source of connection to the cosmological forces of nature (Strassberg 1994).

In Imperial times such travels normally did not go beyond the borders of the Middle Kingdom. In today's globalized world it would however be very surprising if the merging of postmodern consumption styles and the traditional wanderlust of the Chinese would not create a strong and long-lasting demand for international travel.

It can therefore be assumed that even if the three decades of almost uninterrupted double-digit economic growth come to an end or at least seriously encounter some of the major problems of China like environmental degradation, an aging society and the less-than-collectivistic mindset of a generation of single child supposed to create a civil society, the number of outbound tourists from China will continue to rise.

The share of the source market China can also be expected to rise further on global terms as the UNWTO projected long-term increase of 4% for world tourism will even with the conservative 9% growth rate of the State Council planning be outpaced and lead to a 7% share of world tourism in 2014. If spending is growing by 9% year-on-year for the next five years, China will overtake France, if it will grow with the same rate as 2005-2009 in the next quinquennium, China will reach the second place as tourism global spender.

Tourism, and especially outbound tourism, will remain strongly connected to the overall political and economical development of China. Inside the country the availability of outbound travel to a growing part of the Chinese society will be used as an indicator for the successful building of a *xiaokang* (basically well-off) society. In the relations with other countries, the Chinese government will try to continue to use the spending power of its citizens either as a tool to illustrate the "soft power" of China towards industrialised countries or as an instrument of foreign aid policy towards developing countries.

The United States and Canada were finally included into the ADS system in 2009, which makes it more likely to be abolished altogether rather sooner than later now that all major and most minor destinations have acquired Approved Destination Status. Other regulations regarding the authorisation to organise outbound tours have also been relaxed.

In the 15 years since 1995 the growing group of affluent urban Mainland Chinese citizens have been successful in getting access to almost all countries in the world, most of the times being a step ahead of the government attempts of regulating and channelling the growth of outbound travel. The biggest challenge for the Chinese government will be to develop new and more modern ways of keeping the ability to instrumentalise China's outbound tourism for its domestic and international policy goals.

A Brief Chronology of Chinese outbound tourism 1995-2010

1995	Start of systematic collection of statistical data on outbound tourism, figures shown 7.1 million outbound travellers. Introduction of five-day working week.
1996	First distinction of travel agencies in China. Only those agencies label as International Travel Agencies (ITAs) are allowed to organise outbound tourism.
1997	Proclamation of "Provisional Regulation on the Management of Outbound Travel by Chinese Citizens at Their Own Expense" Beginning of chaotic stage with zero fee tours, no real product development and service providers' low quality practices. Approved Destination Status (ADS) for Australia.
1998	First edition of the China International Travel Mart (CITM) in Shanghai.
1999	Start of the "Golden Weeks", which gives the population 114 days of official rest.
2000	Beijing citizens' per capita disposable income up to US$1,253.
2001	First ADS agreement in Europe signed with Malta.
2002	Hong Kong government abolishes the limit for the number of visitors from Mainland Chinese. First African country, Egypt, granted with the ADS.
2003	SAR's outbreak reduces the number of Chinese travellers.
2004	Intense growth in the approval of countries with ADS. Total of 91, compared to 18 in 2001.
2005	More ADS countries translate in an increase of travel agencies, from the 16,846 registered agencies in China, 672 are certified to handle outbound travellers.
2006	First books on backpacking or individual tourism available in Chinese.
2007	From the honeymoon period to more positive, government policy, segmentation of the market, ADS groups and sophisticated travels. Adjustment of numbers of legal holidays by replacing the Mayday "Golden weeks" with several traditional Chinese festivals upgraded to public holidays.
2008	In June, USA finally gets inside the Approved Destination Status system, followed by similar arrangement with Taiwan in July.
2009	Chinese Outbound Tourism reports positive growth despite global economic crisis and H1N1 scare with a 3.6% increase with 47.5 million border crossings by Mainland Chinese citizens. Number of ADS countries reaches 137.
2010	The mood in China is optimistic and tourism has been positioned as a top priority in the government's agenda.

References

Arlt, Wolfgang G. (2006): *China's Outbound Tourism*. London/New York.

Arlt, Wolfgang G. (2010a): 2009 figures confirm importance of Chinese outbound travellers for global tourism development. In: *COTRI Newsletter* No. 16. 01.02.2010. http://www.china-outbound.com.

Arlt, Wolfgang G. (2010b): Selbsterkundung in der Fremde. Nationalismus und Identitätsfindung im chinesischen Tourismus. In: Soboll, Anne (2010) (ed.): *Deutschland als Incoming Destination*. München/Wien (in press).

CNTA (2004) (ed.): *The Yearbook of China Tourism Statistics 2004*. Beijing.

CNTA (2010): *Tourism Statistics*. 01.02.2010. http://en.cnta.gov.cn/.

Guthrie, Doug. (2006): *China and Globalization*. Abingdon.

Henson, Robert (2008): *Climate Change*. London/New York.

Lipman, Geoffrey (2009): *Milestone in China's Tourism Policy*. 01.02.2010. http://www.unwto.org.

Palmer, Catherine (1998): Tourism and the Symbols of Identity. In: *Tourism Management*, 20, S. 313-321.

Pye, Lucian W. (1996): How China's Nationalism was Shanghaied. In: Unger, Jonathan (Hrsg.): *Chinese Nationalism*. Armonk, S. 86-112.

Renmin Ribao (2009): *China's outbound investment to exceed FDI for first time in 2009*. 01.02.2010. http://english.peopledaily.com.cn.

Rosen, Daniel H., Hanemann, Thilo (2009): *China's Changing Outbound Foreign Direct Investment Profile: Drivers and Policy Implications*. Peterson Institute for International Economics Paper PB09. 01.02.2010. http://www.iie.com/publications/pb/pb09-14.pdf.

Steinmetz, Thomas (2007): China "red tourism" boom said good for economy. *eTurbo-News*. 01.02.2010. http://www.eturbonews.com/460.

Strassberg, Richard E. (1994): *Inscribed Landscapes: Travel Writing from Imperial China*. Berkeley.

Tse, Tony Sze Ming (2009): *Forces shaping the trends and patterns of China's outbound international tourist flows*. PhD thesis School of Tourism and Hospitality Management, Southern Cross University.

UNWTO (2009: *UNWTO Tourism Highlights 2009 Edition.* 02.02.2010. http://www.unwto.org/facts/eng/pdf/highlights/UNWTO_Highlights09_en _LR.pdf

UNWTO (2010):UNWTO *World Tourism Barometer.* 02.02.2010. http://www.unwto.org/facts/eng/pdf/barometer/UNWTO_Barom10_1_en _excerpt.pdf

World Bank (2010): 01.02.2010. http://www.worldbank.org.

Xu, Gang (1999): *Tourism and Local Economic Development in China. Case Studies of Guilin, Suzhou and Beidaihe.* Richmond.

Zhang, Guangrui (1989): Ten Years of Chinese Tourism: Profile and Assessment. In *Tourism Management*, 10: 1: 51–62.

Zhao, Xinluo (1994): Barter Tourism Along the China-Russia Border. *In Annals of Tourism Research*, 21: 2: 401–403.

China's Outbound Tourism to Germany

Rainer Fugmann & Gerlis Fugmann

1.   The Changing Global Tourism

Globalization causes more and more people to travel worldwide. The World Tourism Organization (UNWTO) predicts that in 2020 more than 1.6 billion people will be travelling internationally – a triplication within a quarter of a century (UNWTO 2000, 10). At the same time, global travel has been subject to considerable structural changes in the recent past. While the majority of international travellers had initially been generated from the traditional origin markets in the western hemisphere (mainly Europe and North America), it is due to a demographic and economic saturation of demand in these markets, that the "new emerging markets" in Asia have gained importance for the international tourism economy.

"For this reason, tourism is developing culturally and geographically from a colonial one-way street with defined role assignments of both host and visitor to a "two-way-traffic" where all parties involved play temporarily both roles."[22]

Furthermore, the structure of German incoming tourism is facing considerable changes. Domestic tourism and its share of 80% of the total number of overnight stays in Germany, still dominates the German tourism industry. However, roughly 55 million international overnight stays in 2008 (an increase of 11 million since 2004), prove that inbound tourism is gaining more and more importance. Within Europe, it is mainly the new markets in Eastern Europe that develop to be strong pillars of the tourism destination Germany. The traditional overseas origin markets like Japan and the United States had to suffer a loss in market shares in the German incoming tourism in the recent past. Alternatively, it is the global future markets like India, the Arabic Gulf states and China that establish themselves not only potentially as lucrative origin markets,

---

[22] Arlt 2004, 8 [translated from German by the author].

but they were also able to continually expand their market position over the last few years.

The results of the changing scheme of international tourism are besides promising potentials, the emergence of new challenges for the international tourism industry. The interaction with the "new" stakeholders and their specific wishes, needs and patterns of behaviour requires a far-reaching rethinking of and adaptation to as well as an examination of the changed reality.

2. The Relevance of Chinese Outbound Tourism for the Destination Germany

Since the beginning of the century, the attention of tourism experts in Germany and around the globe has turned towards the source market China. This China euphoria was triggered in 2000 by a forecast of the World Tourism Organization, expecting that in 2020 100 million Chinese will be travelling abroad (UNWTO 2003, 9).[23] China would therefore replace Germany in the medium term as the world leader in travel.

Accordingly, the reaction of German and other European tourism experts was very enthusiastic when they were able to receive the status of an approved travel destination by the Chinese authorities. This was arranged on a bilateral basis for Germany in 2002 and again in 2004 for the whole Schengen region. Reactions of the German media clearly reflected this euphoria: "We reckon that in the course of time every Chinese will once visit Germany"[24] [translated from German by the author], "China is the last big growth market worldwide" (FAZ 2003, 15 [translated from German by the author]) and "the cityscape of Paris, Munich or Heidelberg will be affected significantly by Chinese in the future" (FAZ 2003, 15 [translated from German by the author]).

Contrary to expectations, an evaluation that goes beyond the sheer numeric potential of China outbound tourism turns out to be more critical in many cases. Additionally, although only a few years have passed since the initial euphoria, unfavourable headlines begin to dominate

---

[23] By now it seems realistic to assume that the number of 100 million Chinese tourists will be reached already in 2015.

[24] Spiegel Online, http://www.spiegel.de/wirtschaft/0,1518,276557,00.html, 05.07.2007 (the former German chancellor Gerhard Schröder was cited here).

German media, like "the Chinese mafia is using visa for trafficking"[25] [translated from German by the author]), "cultures clash" (Der Spiegel 2006, 80[translated from German by the author]), "with the sale of voyages alone we will hardly be able to earn money"[26] [translated from German by the author] or "in Chinese travel guides, travellers to Europe are advised not to chatter too loud, and to refrain from spitting on the ground or to burp in restaurants"[27] [translated from German by the author].

The change in perception of Chinese incoming tourism from an almost naïve euphoria to a relatively profound disillusionment is an expression of a conflict that emerged between the promising potentials of the Chinese incoming tourism on the one side and numerous, so far unsolved obstacles on the other.

2.1 Extent and Volume of Chinese incoming tourism in Germany

According to statistics released by the German National Tourist Board, Europe was able to attract 3.8 million Chinese tourists (excluding Hongkong and Macao) in 2007 which is equivalent to a market share of 28%. In a European comparison, Germany ranks in second place with a market share of 14% of all arrivals of Chinese tourists in Europe, behind Russia and followed by Italy, Great Britain and France (DZT 2009, 16). To what extent Russia should be counted towards statistics of Chinese tourism in Europe is debatable, as Russia has maintained booming border traffic with the People's Republic for decades.

In 2008, approximately 420.000 arrivals of Chinese visitors have been registered in Germany, generating about 950.000 overnight stays (see Fig. 1). The volume of overnight stays increased since the receipt of ADS status in 2002 by approximately 70%, however it should be mentioned that the current economic crisis will likely leave its mark on Chinese incoming tourism in Germany. Trend evaluations for 2009 will also be influenced negatively by the fear of a possible swine flu pandemic.

---

[25] SZ, http://www.sueddeutsche.de/politik/594/402375/text/, 25.12.2007.

[26] SZ, http://www.sueddeutsche.de/reise/artikel/944/81863/text/, 05.10.2007.

[27] Focus Online, http://www.focus.de/kultur/leben/voelkerkunde-seltsames-doitse-lan_aid_226159.html, 13.02.2008.

A negative trend regarding the development of Chinese tourism is noticeable in the average duration of stays in Germany. While in 1994 Chinese visitors stayed on average 2.9 nights, this number has dropped to currently 2.2 nights. This could be explained by a shift in the purpose of travel a decrease in the percentage of Chinese business travellers who generally stay longer, and an increase in Chinese leisure tourists who tend to stay shorter. In comparison with many other European countries, Chinese business travel still maintains a special role for the destination Germany. Approximately 49% of Chinese visitors are listed as business travellers (DZT 2009, 13), what can be traced back primarily to two reasons: the popularity of Germany as a location for international trade exhibitions and the intensive economic linkages between the two national economies.

Despite all difficulties, the German National Tourist Board forecasts that China will, until 2015, replace Japan as the most important Asian origin market in Germany with approximately 2 million overnight stays.[28]

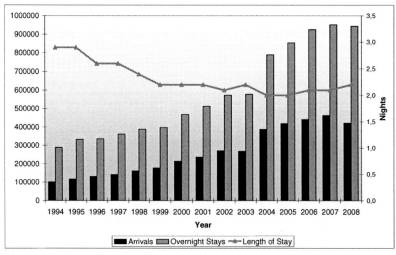

Fig. 1: Development of arrivals, overnight stays and duration of stays of Chinese tourists in Germany[29]

---

[28] Touristik Presse, http://www.touristikpresse.net/news/14585, 02.08.2008.
[29] Statistisches Bundesamt Germany 2007 [calculations by the author].

Overnight stays of Chinese visitors concentrate on the German states of Bavaria, Hesse, North Rhine-Westphalia, Baden-Württemberg, Rhineland-Palatinate and Berlin (see Fig. 2). These states stand out for having both locations for trade exhibition which are important for Chinese business travel as well as internationally well-known tourism highlights. Additionally an infrastructural component is contributing to the advantage of location, as Frankfurt and Munich are equipped with international airports that have regular scheduled flight connections with China. Furthermore, another influencing factor is that these states are situated along tourism "highways", which Chinese tourists generally travel on within Germany. The significance of this geographic distinctiveness can be demonstrated with Berlin as an example: despite its popularity in China, overnight stays are below the average for Chinese tourists. Large parts of northern and eastern Germany are from a Chinese traveller's perspective, touristic no man's land.

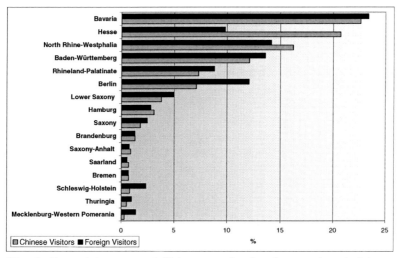

Fig. 2: Overnight stays of Chinese and other international visitors in the German states in 2006[30]

---

[30] DZT 2009, 17; Statistisches Bundesamt Germany 2007 [calculations by the author].

51

Additionally, a concentration of overnight stays in only a few big cities can be noticed. In 2007, 22% of all overnight stays of Chinese visitors were allotted to Munich and Frankfurt. The so-called „magic cities"[31] represented together 42% of all Chinese overnight stays in Germany (DZT 2009, 17).

2.2 Characteristics of the China Outbound Tourism and their Implications for the Destination Germany

The development and distribution of the numbers for arrivals and overnight stays of Chinese tourists in Germany reflect the real market structure. However, hidden behind these dry statistics are human beings, thus giving reason to discuss specific characteristics of the China outbound tourism and its implications on the destination Germany in more detail.

2.2.1 Travel Regulations

First and foremost, different travel regulations determine the development of Chinese outbound travel, both on the Chinese and German or European side.

On the Chinese side, primarily conditions that are incorporated in the "Approved Destination Status" system (ADS system) have to be mentioned. The basic idea of the ADS system is to create the possibility for Chinese travellers to obtain a valid ADS-visa without major passport or visa formalities through approved travel agencies. In theory, according to the framework conditions listed in a Memorandum of Understanding between the People's Republic of China and the respective host country, this visa enables the travellers to travel in a relatively uncomplicated way to the "approved" destination. In reality, the situation is as follows: members of Chinese tourist groups have to travel to and from Schengen countries as a group of minimum five people. The group has to travel according to a predefined travel program and has to be accompanied by a guide at all times.[32] Under these circumstances, individual foreign travel of Chinese citizens is not possible or only in a very limited way.

---

[31] The marketing network „magic cities" encompasses the cities of Frankfurt, Munich, Berlin Cologne, Düsseldorf, Hamburg, Stuttgart, Hannover and Dresden.

[32] http://www.dihk.de/index.html?/inhalt/themen/branchen/tourismus/china_tourismus.htm, 25.07.2007.

These regulations are increased by another problem of great controversy: after published reports about members of Chinese tourist groups illegally trying to disappear during their travel, Germany has tightened the guidelines for the simplified ADS visa process on its side since early 2005. Germany considered itself especially endangered, as just for 2004, about two thirds of all ADS visas approved by EU-countries in China were issued by German consulates.[33] The new guidelines arrange for a certain percentage of applicants, regardless of their place of residence, to show up at the German consulate in person before and sometimes even a second time after the end of their journey. Additionally, all changes to the approved travel route have to be reported to authorities immediately; false information reported by the travel agency is strictly punished.

However, the crucial factor is not the types of restrictions but the negative impact chain that they trigger. It is important to keep in mind that the destination Germany is in direct competition to other Schengen countries that do not apply such strict interpretations of the visa formalities. The inevitable result is that Chinese travel agencies try to let their customers to travel around Europe through other Schengen countries due to the strict German visa rules. This, in turn, means that touristic service providers in Germany tend to profit less from Chinese incoming tourism. Although other Schengen countries have tightened their visa regulations in the mean time as well, the goal should be to introduce the same standards in all Schengen countries. This would avoid that some countries profit more from the China business than others, due to more lax visa regulations.

2.2.2 Travel Inexperience

The majority of Chinese outbound travellers, especially the long-distance travellers, are still considered to be relatively inexperienced in travel. Travel inexperience, language barriers and a resulting insecurity towards the "other", along with only elusive cultural reasons, add to the fact that Chinese travel groups usually travel a destination in a "channelled" way. Even though they move in another country, they remain in their own world. Individuals hardly leave their group; groups tend to take their meals together in Chinese restaurants. Clusters of Chinese-owned service

---

[33] SZ, http://www.sueddeutsche.de/politik/476/402257/text/, 02.10.2007.

providers directed specifically towards Chinese clientele develop around tourist attractions that are popular among Chinese tourists.

Factors like the appearance in groups, the limited experience of many Chinese tourists with customs from other cultures as well as an enormous knowledge deficit on the part of many German hosts in the handling of specific behaviour patterns of the Chinese visitors can lead to sometimes bizarre problems in gastronomy and the hotel business. This was described very emotionally by a hotel owner in Trier: "There are about ten people coming to eat and only five order food and then they pass around plates. That is not possible. I've also talked to other hotel owners. They also don't want Chinese anymore. They also say: with those table manners! You can't seat the Chinese with other guests. You can't expect them to put up with that." (Interview 04.10.2007 [translated by the author]). On the one hand this quote shows that an inter-cultural understanding and mutual courtesy are essential if the Chinese incoming tourism should be developed into a lucrative business area. On the other hand the quote clarifies that the general potentials of the China tourism for the gastronomy and retail industry sector in Germany should be relatively kept in perspective.

At this point, the necessity to distinguish between the typical package tourist and the growing number tourists that are experienced and quality-oriented regarding the motives for and the destination of travel should be mentioned. Despite the lack of exact data, the ratio between both groups is estimated to be 90:10 in case of the sample Germany. No changes are expected in the near future regarding this finding as still large numbers of inexperienced potential package tourists are waiting to go on their first travel. Surely, the outbound tourism in China is still in its infancy. Nevertheless, in its first approach, it can be interpreted to be, and will be in the future to an even larger extent, a reflection of the increasingly diversified Chinese society. This will not, however, eliminate that in the future specific basic patterns and peculiarities of Chinese tourists will still appear to be generalized as "different" from a western perspective.

2.2.3 Price Orientation

The People's Republic of China is currently experiencing a constant transformation from a planned towards a market-oriented economy, reflected as well in the tourism sector. Large parts of the emerging tourism market are still being regulated and are only partially privatized. Clear contours are lacking in a network of business competition between a large number of old and new operators, whereas foreign tour operators are largely excluded from the outbound tourism business.

All this contributes to the fact that competition between the Chinese operators — having limited experience and thus offering customers similar programs — is primarily based on the factor price. Diversification of offers with an emphasis on quality is only achieved slowly.[34]

The lack of reliable premium brands, a large homogeneity of the offers and very little market transparency, in addition to the travel inexperience and limited economic resources[35] of many Chinese customers, causes them to select from the variety of operators according to the factor price. This is intensified by a strong price orientation of Chinese customers in general which might be explained by their mentality or cultural history.

All of this leads to an increasing downward spiral of the offer price. It is not surprising that the average price for a 10 to 15-day trip to Europe, including flight, accommodation and transport on site, only ranges between 1.000 to 2.000 Euros (Schuler & Liu 2007, 67).

The Chinese price orientation makes the business area less lucrative for incoming agencies and service providers in Germany and other destinations. For example, Chinese travel operators expect a 3 to 4-star hotel to lower its offer to 30 or even 20 Euros. Many touristic service providers engaged in China tourism can expect high sales volumes but profits are generally low due to low margins.

The low price level is usually accompanied by low standards in quality. Hidden and exorbitant additional charges as well as specific misinformation concerning location and amenities of the hotels also contribute to the negative impact chain as an attempt to amortize cost on the basis of provisions. The travel inexperience of Chinese tourists as well as their

---

[34] China Daily, http://www.chinadaily.com.cn/english/doc/2006-02/04/content_516983.htm, 02.10.2007.

[35] The low flexibility in prices results from the average monthly family income of 82% of all Chinese outbound tourists being less than 1.900 Euros, roughly the equivalent of a Europe trip (UNWTO 2006, 11). Additionally, there is a basic tendency to budget the amount that was saved on a cheaper offer for incidental expenses like shopping.

resulting dependency on the travel guide is quite often being exploited and misused.

Consequences of these business practices are a decrease in visitor satisfaction and damages to the public image of a destination.

2.2.4 Travel route

As a result of limited financial resources, a Europe trip is considered to be very exclusive and connected with high prestige for the majority of Chinese package tourists.

Another important factor is that due to the travel inexperience, the majority of Chinese travellers look upon the destination Europe as a whole. Borders within Europe are not important — the diversity of Europe appears as one entity. "(...) Europe is seen as one destination that offers the opportunity to visit many different countries in close proximity but with varied cultures and attractions (...)" (Arlt 2006, 174). Despite existing stereotypes of different countries[36] and especially different cities[37], it is the diversity of Europe that is being valued as a unique feature. These aspects allow for drawing conclusions on the travel motive and habit of Chinese travellers to Europe. The priority is to visit as many of the touristic highlights as possible in the shortest time possible. This is realized mostly in the form of round trips by bus along the previously mentioned touristic highways, in hardly ever varying travel routes focusing on European metropolises. Germany is therefore for the majority of leisure tourists just a partial destination within a Europe trip. For that reason, the spatial impact of Chinese leisure tourism in Germany regarding the criteria duration of stay and choice of travel route, has to be kept in perspective.

---

[36] France for example is considered to be romantic and elegant, Italy is brought in connection with the Romans, Switzerland is considered to be rich, clean and the home of clocks, etc (Spiegel Online, http://wissen.spiegel.de/wissen/dokument/dokument.html?id=52559411&top=SPIEGEL, 14.08.2007).

[37] Paris is considered to be romantic and the home of the Eiffel tower, Munich is the beer capital and Rome is associated with culture (Arlt 2006, 178).

2.3 "Anomalies" of the Chinese incoming tourism in Germany

The majority of Chinese package tourists primarily visit classical highlights like Munich, Rome or Paris along a "race track" through Europe. Despite that, smaller destinations in Germany can sporadically profit to some extent from the Chinese incoming tourism. They offer promising approaches for a specific development of the Chinese travel market. The common element is the specific emphasis of their unique features on the origin market China. Mainly characteristics that attract Chinese tourists (e.g. prestige, authenticity, myths, brands and shopping) or that enables them to connect something familiar with it (e.g. Karl Marx, cuckoo clocks, Hugo Boss, the Pied Piper of Hamelin) are highlighted. Setting these reference points for orientation seems to be essential in regards to the travel inexperience of many Chinese visitors. Some of these "anomalies" will be discussed further below.

Trier

The destination Trier is the most well-known "anomaly" with regards to the Chinese incoming tourism in Germany. With about 40,000 overnight stays in 2006, the Chinese tourists are the second largest foreign visitors group behind the Dutch. Trier is primarily focusing on the factor prestige. As the birthplace of Karl Marx — so to speak the founding father of the People's Republic of China — the city's degree of popularity is very high in China. Despite the new orientation of the People's Republic on an economic and political level, Trier succeeded in establishing itself as a fixed point on many touristic travel routes within Europe. Other initiatives of introducing other attractions of Trier to Chinese visitors (e.g. Roman heritage) have been unsuccessful so far.

Metzingen

The city of Metzingen near Stuttgart managed to establish itself firmly with the theme "retail" as a destination for day tourists for the Chinese incoming tourism in Germany. Chinese outbound tourists regularly tend to reserve a high percentage of their travel expenses for shopping. The percentage of shopping expenses as to the overall expenses is fluctuating between 15% to 50%[38] (King, Dwyer & Prideaux 2006, 137). The factors price[39], image, product security as well as the Chinese tradition of making gifts serve as explanations for the disproportionally high consumer expenses of Chinese tourists for shopping. According to information by "Global Refund", about 4.6% of all Germany-wide "tax-free" shopping expenses of Chinese tourists in 2006 were made in Metzingen. Metzingen ranks on sixth place in the list of the most popular shopping destinations of Chinese tourists in Germany, before cities like Hamburg, Stuttgart or Nuremberg (DZT 2009, 17). At this, the outlet city Metzingen can ideally serve the factors price, brand and image — whereby it is important to mention the special popularity of the brand Hugo Boss.

Titisee

Another example is the success story of Titisee-Neustadt in the Black Forest. The city was able to position itself as a destination for Chinese day tourists — even though on a smaller scale — through the attractive marketing of two images: "romance" on the basis of the "Magic Black Forest" concept; and "authenticity" on the basis of the worldwide well-known cuckoo clock. The specific combination of an "authentic" product within a "romantic" surrounding is the recipe for success of this Black Forest destination.

Hameln

Hameln is profiting from the surprisingly high level of popularity of German fairy tales in China. As part of the 'German fairy-tale route', the destination marketing is focusing on the figure of the 'Pied Piper of Hamelin'. Here, the factor of success is the affinity of many Chinese to myths and legends. As a result of the travel inexperience of most Chinese package tourists, they want to visit as many attractions as possible on their trip. A special destination like Hameln can therefore only be marketed as a small subset of a greater whole. For such a destination to

---

[38] China Daily, http://www.chinadaily.com.cn/english/doc/2006-02/04/content_516983.htm, 02.10.2007.

[39] In China, comparatively high fees and taxes are charged on luxury articles. Taxes and fees on e.g. brand-names watches are currently 30% and cosmetics 50%. Similar rates apply for diverse fashion articles, jewellery etc. (China Daily, http://www.chinadaily.com.cn/cndy/2006-12/28/content_769323.htm, 02.10.2007).

get a bigger piece of the cake, the target groups of experienced and quality-oriented tourists or follow-up travellers are the only ones where chances of success will first and foremost be seen.

2.4 Critical Evaluation of the Potentials of Chinese Incoming Tourism for the Destination Germany

In general, it seems to be difficult for Germany to position itself as an independent tourist destination in the origin market China. Above all, an easy comprehensible and unique touristic profile is currently missing. Germany is known in China in particular as a business destination, which is reflected in the previously mentioned high proportion of business travellers. Even though it is also well-known in China for its interesting (intellectual) history[40], as well as images and stereotypes like "romance" and "order", Germany is often — not only in China — equated with the state of Bavaria.

Against this background, the regional diversity with which Germany is advertising itself abroad could be regarded as less beneficial for the young source market China. Specific orientation points are often missing for potential Chinese visitors and especially for the majority of travel inexperienced tourists. Instead of emphasizing the small structured, regional distinctiveness, another path should be chosen for new markets like China. Europe or supranational regions with similar touristic profile could be marketed, for example, as a big destination. One fact should not be ignored: at the end of 2008, almost 140 destinations including the United States had gained the status of approved travel destination for Chinese tourism and within the young source market China, Germany and Europe are direct competitors to other world regions regarding market shares.

---

[40] Especially the old classics like Goethe, Beethoven and the Brothers Grimm are very popular in China. Also the topic 'national socialism' is raising interests among Chinese visitors. Additionally, Germany is considered to be the home of famous inventors, a producer of high-quality products like cars and as the country of the beer (Arlt 2008, 20).

3. Summary and Outlook for the Destination Germany

The Chinese outbound tourism has to be evaluated more critically in many aspects as suggested by the pure observation of numeric potentials. Then again, a one-sided negative portrait of the Chinese outgoing tourism on the basis of some of the problem areas used in this article is not appropriate either. A critical reflection, including a weighing of the "pros and cons" allows to draw the conclusion that the Chinese source market is being presented as "important but over-hyped".[41] On the one hand, on the short and medium term, it is not predictable if the current characteristics, challenges and problem areas will change fundamentally. On the other hand it would be short sighted to not allow a market that is in the process of developing the freedom to make mistakes.

With regards to the destination Germany, the question if China will be an important source market in the future is considered to be less important as the prospects are quite positive. Instead the question has to be asked if Germany is prepared for the needs of the Chinese clientele. In particular, regarding the orientation of touristic infrastructure towards the specific wishes and needs of Chinese visitors, a backlog is noticeable. If Germany wants to position itself on the long run as a destination for the origin market China, this has to be overcome fast.

---

[41] Financial Times, http://search.ft.com/ftArticle?queryText=Yuk+visa+rules&y= 6&aje=false&x=8&id=050726000809&ct=0, 02.10.2007 (citation of Tom Jenkins, Director of the 'European Tour Operator Association').

References

Arlt, Wolfgang G. (2004): Chinesischer Outbound-Tourismus in Deutschland: Entwicklung – Perspektiven – Herausforderungen. In: Maschke, Joachim (Hg.): *Jahrbuch für Fremdenverkehr 2004*. München. 7-34.

Arlt, Wolfgang G. (2006): *China's Outbound Tourism*. London/New York.

Arlt, Wolfgang G. (2008): Entwicklung des Outbound Tourismus in China aus europäischer Sicht. In: Arlt, Wolfgang G./Freyer, Walter (Hg.): *Deutschland als Reiseziel chinesischer Touristen*. München. 7-21.

China Daily (Hg.) (2006a): *New duty levied on luxuries*. 02.10.2007. http://www. chinadaily.com.cn/cndy/2006-12/28/content_769323.htm.

China Daily (Hg.) (2006b): *Outbound travelling jumps 50-fold in 20 years*. http://www.chinadaily.com.cn/english/doc/2006-02/04/content _516983.htm 02.10.2007.

Der Spiegel (Hg.) (2006): Zwei Nächte in Deutschland. In: *Der Spiegel*, 33/2006, 80.

Deutscher Bundestag (Hg.) (2006): *Drucksache 16/2221*. http://dip21. bundestag.de/dip21/btd/16/022/1602221.pdf 14.03.2007.

DZT (Hg.) (2009): *Marktinformation China / Hongkong*. http://www. deutschland-extranet.de/pdf/MI_China_HongKong_2009.pdf 15.06.2009.

EU (Hg.) (2004): *Memorandum of Understanding between the National Tourism Administration of the People's Republic of China and the European Community on visa related issues concerning tourist groups from the People's Republic of China (ADS)*. http://www.dihk.de/index.html?/inhalt/themen/branchen/tourismus/china_t ourismus.htm 25.07.2007.

FAZ (Hg.) (2003): Die Chinesen werden die neuen Reiseweltmeister. In: *FAZ*, 22.12.2003, 15.

Financial Times (Hg.) (2005): *Tourism warning as China relaxes visa rules*. http://search.ft.com/ftArticle?queryText=Yuk+visa+rules&y=6&aje= false&x=8&id=050726000809&ct=0 02.10.2007.

FOCUS Online (Hg.) (2007): *Seltsames Doi Tse Lan*.
http://www.focus.de/kultur/leben/voelkerkunde-seltsames-doi-tse-lan_aid_226159.html 13.02.2008.

IHT (Hg.) (2005): *The subtle power of Chinese tourists*. http://www.nytimes.com/2005/10/06/world/asia/06iht-tourism.html?_r=1 02.10.2007.

King, Brian/Dwyer, Larry/Prideaux, Bruce (2006): An Evaluation of Unethical Business Practices in Australia's China Inbound Tourism Market. In: *International Journal of Tourism Research*, 8: 2: 127-142.

People's Daily (Hg.) (2006): *Europe "unprepared" for Asian tourists*. http://english.people.com.cn/200611/07/print20061107_319021.html 02.10.2007.

Schuler, Alexander/Liu, Yina (2008): Outbound-Reiseveranstalter in China: Entwicklung und Struktur von organisierten Reisen nach Deutschland. In: Arlt, Wolfgang G./Freyer, Walter (Hg.): *Deutschland als Reiseziel chinesischer Touristen*. München. 59-72.

Spiegel Online (Hg.) (2003): *Achtung, die Chinesen kommen*. http://www. spiegel.de/wirtschaft/0,1518,276557,00.html 05.07.2007.

Spiegel Online (Hg.) (2007): *Expedition Fern-West* http://wissen.gel.de/wissen/dokument/dokument.html?id=52559411&top= SPIEGEL 14.08.2007.

SZ (Hg.) (2005a): *Chinesische Mafia nutzt Visa für Schleusergeschäft*. http://www.sueddeutsche.de/politik/594/402375/text/ 25.12.2007.

SZ (Hg.) (2005b): *BND warnt Kanzleramt vor chinesischer Schleuser-Mafia*. http://www.sueddeutsche.de/politik/476/402257/text/ 02.10.2007.

SZ (Hg.) (2006): *Süßsauere Ferien*. http://www.sueddeutsche.de/ reise/artikel/944/81863/text/ 05.10.2007.

Touristik Presse (Hg.) (2008): *Prognose Deutschland-Tourismus: DZT erhöht Incoming-Prognose auf 66 Millionen Übernachtungen für 2015*. http://www. touristikpresse.net/news/14585 02.08.2008.

UNWTO (Hg.) (2000): *Tourism 2020 Vision Volume 3: East Asia and the Pacific*. Madrid.

UNWTO (Hg.) (2003): *Chinese Outbound Tourism*. Madrid.

UNWTO (Hg.) (2006): *China: The Asia and the Pacific Intra-Regional Outbound Series*. Madrid.

Chinese outbound tourism to Mexico, what to do to attract them?

Berenice Aceves

1. Introduction

Tourism is one of the most important economic sectors for Mexico. According to official figures, the industry's contribution to GDP was an average of 8.2% during the 2003-2006 periods, employing 2.4 million people directly and indirectly, which translates to 6.75% of the total employed population in Mexico[42]. Through the years this activity has contributed to elevate Mexicans quality of life and has been an engine for the nation's economy.

An opportunity to increase the tourist international arrivals to Mexico is the attraction of emerging markets, one of them being the Chinese outbound market. Due to the "reform and opening" policy introduced by Deng Xiaoping in 1978, China began its transformation to a key player in the global scene. Thirty years later, results can be perceived in different sectors, the economic activities changed from agricultural-based to industrial; the country has enjoyed an average economic growth of 9% which translates to higher disposable income and better life conditions for its population. Even now, in times of economic crisis, China has shown a recovery growth of 7.9% in the second quarter of 2009 and expects 8% or more by the end of the year[43].

As a result recreation activities have developed satisfactorily among Chinese citizens. The open gates will allow China to become the fourth inbound tourism market and a future important outbound source market capable of sending an estimated of 100 million tourists by 2015. While in 1995 only 7,139 exits were recorded; 2008 saw 45.8 million Chinese crossing the borders. However, from this figure almost 70-75% of those crossing the borders went to neighbouring Hong Kong and Macao (Spe-

---

[42] INEGI, 20.02.2009,
   http://dgcnesyp.inegi.org.mx/cgi-win/bdiecoy.exe/739?c=12601.
[43] China Daily, 20.07.2009,
   http://www.chinadaily.com.cn/bizchina/2009-07/16/content_8435594.htm.

cial Administrative Regions, SARs). The China National Tourism Administration (CNTA) has forecasted 50 million tourists travelling by the end of 2009. This is a 9% growth, but a decrease of 3% when compared to an impressive 12% rise in 2008[44].

Chinese citizens are relatively new on the travel scene, and while abroad they enjoy luxurious shopping and practice the Chinese philosophy of "economize in home, but get enough for the road". Gaining social status, while travelling across cultures, is a primordial motivation. Status is attained solely through the views of one's surrounding group, and criteria vary between groups (Blok 2002, 10).

Some pull factors, referring to the importance of destination attributes, are shown in a study (conducted by Kim et al. 2005, 219) reporting safety, beauty of the scenery, well-equipped tourism facilities, different cultural/historical resources and good weather as the top five. Quality is also an increasing characteristic for the upper end of the market of Chinese travellers. They are willing and able to spend more if they get high quality services – quality according to specific Chinese customs, values and demands[45].

The Chinese governments' loosening of restrictions has contributed to the increased number of travellers. By creating the Approved Destination Status (ADS), Chinese authorities have controlled the number of leisure tourists going out of mainland China and clearly establish the places they are able to visit. For nations willing to attract Chinese tourists, a first step was getting the ADS. As of 2009, almost all major destinations have entered into ADS or similar agreements. After that, destinations have to focus on specific product development, quality offer and promotion. The increasing global awareness of the Chinese outbound market has generated major efforts of promotion of foreign destinations in mainland China; National Tourism Offices activities, interesting articles in magazines, national media coverage are some examples. According to a study conducted in Shanghai in 2006 (Sparks & Pan 2008, 10), television programs play an important role in how Chinese people learn

---

[44] CNTA, 08.01.2009,
    http://en.cnta.gov.cn/html/2009-1/2009-1-8-17-46-75892.html.
[45] COTRI, 15.04.2009,
    http://www.china-outbound.com/index.php?option=com_content&view=
    article&id=73&Itemid=73.

about target destinations. The sample also reported fairly high levels of Internet use.

Mexico is one of those destinations pursuing to attract a growing number of Chinese outbound tourists. The current article uses results from the author's master thesis research period 2006-2008, both in Mexico and China, in order to identify what constrains Chinese outbound tourists from travel to Mexico, and what actions can Mexico undertake to attract them.

2. Importance of the tourism sector in Mexico

In terms of tourism, for Mexico's economy the industry represents the third main economic activity just after oil and manufacture. In 2008, over 22.6 million visitors came to Mexico; it is positioned as the number ten destination in international tourists arrivals, the list being headed by France, United States, Spain, China, Italy, United Kingdom, Ukraine, Turkey and Germany (SECTUR 2009a, 89).

International	Year				Growth %		
Visitors	2005	2006	2007	2008	08 - 05	08 - 06	08 - 07
Visitors	103.146	97.701	92.233	91,462	-11,3	-6,4	-0,8
Tourists	21.915	21.353	21.424	22,637	3,3	6,0	5,9
Internal	12.534	12.608	13.010	13,300	6,1	5,5	2,7
Borders	9.381	8.745	8.414	9,338	-0,5	6,8	11,0
Excursionist	81.239	76.348	70.810	68,825	-15,3	-9,9	-2,8
Borders	74.524	69.832	63.995	62,394	-16,3	-10,7	-2,5
Cruiseship	6.707	6.516	6.815	6,431	-4,1	-1,3	-5,6

**Fig. 1: International visitors to Mexico, 2004-2008[46]
(thousand people).**

Expenditure by international tourists was 10.8 million dollars in 2008, representing 4.6% more than in 2007. Related to international visitors' expenditure, 2008 registered 13.2 million dollars, 3.4% higher compared to 2007. While visiting Mexico, international tourists' average expenditure was 761 dollars per stay in 2008. Main source markets to Mexico are

---

[46] SECTUR 2009c, 1.

North America and Europe with 74% and 11% participation each. This is followed by the Latin America and Caribbean region that representing 5.4% of the 2008 total.

Mexico is well known for its wide touristic offer. By 2008, 59 tourism destinations are listed by the Mexican Council for the Promotion of Tourism (CPTM by its initials in Spanish). Products are developed according to the following segments: sports and nautic, alternative, business, cultural, health, nature, specialized and tourism for everybody.[47]

The end of 2008 and the first quarter of 2009 has been a difficult period for the Mexican tourism industry, mainly because of the economic recession in the United States, an important source market to Mexico which represents 65.4% of the market; and the H1N1 flu cases reported in Mexico in April and May 2009.

3. Mexico as a travel destination for Chinese tourists

Tourism between Mexico and China started in 1978, 6 years after beginning diplomatic relations both governments signed the Agreement of Touristic Cooperation used mainly for diplomatic and business travel. A second level of cooperation was granted to Mexico with the Approved Destination Status (ADS) in August 2004, formal signing of the Memorandum of Understanding (MoU) was in January 2005. The eight- article document describes the responsibilities of both sides' travel agencies concerning facilitating the arrival of Chinese outbound tourism groups.

By 2008, Mexico had selected 106 authorized travel agencies. During the qualitative research, structure interviews were made to Mexican travel agents with the authorization to receive Chinese tourism. From the survey 12% agencies have organized Chinese tours in Mexico, 41% have made a big effort but with no success and 45% have not made any kind of effort. Currently, the Mexican tourism industry is getting to know the market and believe that promotion has to be done along with the governmental institutions.

---

[47] SECTUR (2008),
    http://www.sectur.gob.mx/wb/sectur/sect_Desarrollo_de_Productos_
    Turisticos, 12.03.2009.

With the objective of promoting Mexico's image in the Chinese tourism market, CPTM opened in 2006 a representative office in Beijing, China.

According to CPTM figures, part of its Winter Analysis of the Chinese Market – 2008 (CPTM 2008, 12), in 2006-2007 the number of Chinese tourists increased 45.4% going from 12,061 to 17,533. The figure is just 24.3% of the 71,857 Japanese tourists that visit Mexico in 2007. Japan is the biggest source market in Asia to Mexico.

Chinese tourists	Years			
	2005	2006	2007	2008
Tourists	10,569	12,061	17,533	20,224
% change	n/a	14.1	45.4	15.3
% from Mexico's total	n/a	0.1	0.1	0.2

Fig. 2: Chinese tourist to Mexico 2005-2008[48]

About the current situation and characteristics of the Chinese outbound tourism to Mexico, CPTM provided the following information:

- Arrivals in 2007 show that 0.1% of international tourists' visits to Mexico are from mainland China. When looking at flight arrivals, China is on the 31st spot nationwide.

- Main sources of tourists are the cities of *Beijing, Shanghai and Guangzhou,* which account for 97% of the total arrivals of 2007. This figure mainly refers to the airports people used to travel to Mexico.

- More than 70% see Mexico City as their principal/final destination, followed by Guadalajara, with 8%. Other important places are Monterrey and Tijuana. Cancun, the second famous destination among the Chinese, is not in this list because Mexico's National Institute of Migration (INM by its initials in Spanish) methodology only in-

---

[48] Flight arrivals. These figures don't include any other way of entrance. *Cabo San Lucas, Cancun, Guadalajara, Ciudad de Mexico, Puerto Vallarta, Cozumel, Hermosillo, León, Mazatlán, Mérida, Monterrey, Acapulco, Zihuatanejo, Huatulco, Tijuana, Zacatecas and Morelia. Source: SIMMT (2009), www.siimt.com, 22.07.2009.

cludes flight arrivals, and most of the tourists first arrived in Mexico City and then continue on to Cancun.

- December, January and February are the busiest months to Mexico, having 24.4% and 22.1% of the total of Chinese tourists, in 2006 and 2007 accordingly.
- Major sales of tourism products are individual and group business 68%, incentives 8%, culture 7%, sea and sun 7%.
- Average price to visit Mexican destinations flying from Beijing is 5,000 USD. Cabo San Lucas is the most expensive destination with an average of 5,526 USD per trip.

Outbound country	Outbound city	Mexico's inbound destination	Average price (USD)
China	Beijing	Cabo San Lucas	5,526
		Ciudad de Mexico	4,725
		Puerto Vallarta	5,013
		Guadalajara	4,776
		Cancun	5,072

Fig. 3: Average tour prices from China to Mexican destinations, 2008[49]

Related to 2008, INM reported 20,224 arrivals of Chinese nationals to Mexico. China's share represented 0.2% of the 22.6 million of total international tourists' arrivals. By the time this article was written, preliminary data shows that 7,235 Chinese tourists entered Mexico from January to May 2009, representing a negative growth of -5.3% compared to the same period in 2008.

When looking at the range of products offered by Mexico's destinations to Chinese tourists with authorized travel agencies, only two all-inclusive package tours were found in China Youth Travel Service (CYTS). One of them included most of the important destination in Mexico (Mexico City, Oaxaca, San Cristobal, Palenque, Campeche, Uxmal, Merida, Chichen Itza, Cancun) and the other linked Mexico with

---

[49] CPTM 2008, 17.

Cuba. Both of them cost more than 4,000 RMB (about 5,600 USD) in 2008.[50]

The product Mexico is in the introduction stage, there are a limited number of arrivals, few packages are offered and both sides of the industry are neither trained enough nor have knowledge about each other's destinations.

A survey was conducted among Chinese visitors to Mexico City, in the summer of 2008, from which the following results can be highlighted: the Chinese visitor once in Mexico City has great expectations and a carefully planned itinerary. This is put together due to previous recommendations from family and friends and from data consulted over the Internet.

In terms of reservation facilities (such as tours, transportation and accommodation) for long distance travel, it is common that the Chinese visitors go to a travel agent instead of booking themselves. The main purpose for travelling is business; it was mentioned that both business and pleasure are usually mixed during their stay. Most travel along with their family, stay over 8 nights and spend an average of 2,000-4,000 USD per stay.

The main activities are: visits to Teotihuacan pyramids, museums (mainly Anthropology Museum), historical downtown and the main square (Zocalo). Some attributes were submitted to evaluation (security, weather, hotel accommodation, hospitality, transportation, travel guides, tourism information, prices, traffic, cleanliness of the city, environment quality and the city as a whole). The visitors were pleased with most features except for security and traffic.

It is important to say that almost all the visitors were pleased with Mexico City, therefore we can expect good recommendations in the future. Some recommendations to improve Mexico City as a destination were working on the safety environment, improving the quality of the roads and reducing time on the traffic jams. Visitors will recommend the city because it is an interesting and historical city, therefore worth visiting.

---

[50] Interview from 16.01.2008 with CYTS, Beijing.

Gender	Age	Marital Status	Profession	Studies	Annual income (USD)
Male (60%) Female (40%)	26 – 35 yrs (44%) 36 – 45 yrs (30%)	Married (78%)	Independent profession (48%)	College (65%)	30,000-45,000 (80%)

Fig. 4: Socio demographic aspects from the Chinese tourist to Mexico City, 2008[51]

Among the subjects in the survey, males constituted the 60% and 44% where aged between 26-35 years. More than half were married (78%) and received an annual income between 30,000-45,000 USD. About 65% have a college education and 48% answer as having an independent profession.

So what do potential Chinese visitors connect with the product "Mexico"? The decision to travel is affected by geographical and psychological factors (personality, worries, motivations), destiny attraction, recommendation influences and marketing efforts (SSAP 2007). During the research time in Beijing, a survey about Mexico's image was conducted amount the main travel industry stakeholders, the following remarks were collected.

- **The association to Mexico mainly consists of two destinations: Mexico City and Cancun.** Those people travelled to Mexico and visited the two cities mainly because of recommendations from family and friends. They mentioned that Mexico, exactly like China, is a multicultural country. Unfortunately, except for these two cities, the rest of the nation is practically unknown.
- **Only business travel and official trips.** Most of the tour operators said that tours are mainly organized for businessmen or government officials. The country still has plenty to do in order to change the image of business only.

[51] Applied survey from 06.2008 to 07.2009.

70

- **Wonderful culture, especially Mayan.** Chinese people know that Mexican culture is a strong piece in the pre-Columbian history, and specially home of the Mayans. This cultural knowledge is mainly recognized among the students involved in Latin-American studies or those who study Spanish.
- **Sports.** Some of them remembered that Mexico was the host of the Olympic Games (without mentioning the specific date of the events). Most of them answered "football". Chinese people are very interested in football; live games of all major leagues are available on Chinese television every week. However, there were no clear names of any famous Mexican football players.

On the other hand, weaknesses were mentioned such as: distance, high prices, no image of the destination and difficult visa procedure. Due to the geographical situation, Mexico will always be expensive and hard to reach. Massive tourists use as reference a visit to Thailand, one of the most famous destinations for Chinese tourists, where for 1,000 RMB (140 USD) they can enjoy a simple tour of 5 days. That price is not even the amount of the flight fee they will encounter when visiting Mexico. Relating to visas the Chinese tourist industry believes it takes a long time, it is even harder than the United States visa procedures and ADS scheme benefits are not used when issuing it.

While analyzing the competitors (Brazil, Peru, Cuba, Jamaica, Egypt, South Africa, countries with a similar tourism offer and characteristics to Mexico), Egypt and Peru seem to be the countries that have benefited from the ADS visa procedure. While Egypt decides to minimize the cost and trust in authorized agencies, Peru bets in a fast visa issue, three days the most. Accordingly, Jamaica sticks to the ADS but they need to obtain the boarding pass of all the travellers after they return to China. Brazil and Mexico still do not use the ADS scheme.

After the overall analysis of the competitors, Mexico is in a favourable position, according to international statistics (Euromonitor 2007, 4). Mexico is the second on Chinese outbound tourist arrivals after Brazil, which received 37,656 visitors in 2006. It is important to notice that these destinations do not consider the Chinese market as a priority, but as introduction or exploration phases. For this reason they have neither invested human nor monetary resources in market research studies.

Moreover, less effort has been made in adapting the infrastructure (signs, training) to the Chinese characteristics.

Country	Issued time (days)	Price RMB	Procedure
Brazil	10 - 15	200	Brazil has not been implemented the ADS. The tourists have to go to the embassy and present all the requirements for individual tourist visa. Some of these requirements are the vaccine against the yellow fever, invitation letter from a Brazilian resident, a certificate of financial competence and a copy of the round-trip air ticket.
Peru	2 - 3	270	Peru benefits from the ADS. The agency asks for a bank deposit that guarantees the return of the tourist.
Cuba	5 - 7	200	No interview is needed. ADS system Visas approve a stay for maximaly30 days.
Jamaica	10 - 15	160	No interview is needed. Issued by the agencies. The boarding pass of each tourist has to be shown to the Jamaican embassy once the Chinese group returned.
Egypt	5	135	No interview is needed. Issued by the agencies.
South Africa	7 - 14	560	Issued by the agencies. Application form A certificate of financial competence.
Mexico	10 - 12	250	Mexico did not obtain the ADS. The tourists have to go to the embassy and present all the requirements for individual tourist visa. Such as an interview, a certificate of financial competence, finger-prints, and more.

Fig. 5: Visa procedure for Chinese citizens in 2008[52]

---

[52] Source: Interviews and information of the tourism representation office of each country, 01.04.2008.

In late August 2008, Prof. Dr. Wolfgang Georg Arlt organized with the help of Dr. Feng Gequn a focus group of Chinese tourism students (more than 100 students) in Ningbo University, located in a big harbour city south-west of Shanghai, which belongs to the second tier Chinese cities. They were asked to respond to the following question: what spontaneously comes to your mind when you think about Mexico? It was an interesting situation and the results were various, though most students had no idea about the destination Mexico, there were about 15 participants who could provide interesting imaginations about Mexico.

Some of them reported about the Mexican Chicken Roll (as can be bought at Kentucky Fried Chicken or McDonald's) and others said that the food in Mexico is too hot and spicy. Other imagination features included the big interesting hats, Mayan culture, maize as a staple food, Spanish-speaking language, their strong football team, a kind of special wine (probably Tequila but this was not specifically mentioned), the neighbourhood to the USA, the high plateau, the desert, the same name of the capital city as the country, the city square, the fat people, and even the Panama canal and so on. Some are not so positive, some are even totally wrong. But the most positive impression is from several girls who said the coach for the Mexican women's water diving team comes from China who helped Mexico to win at least one medal in the 2008 Summer Olympic Games.

The image of Mexico is mostly a piece of "white paper" to the Chinese outbound tourists. A clear image needs to be created, therefore is very important to cater with quality services and make a good impression for those first-time visitors to Mexico.

4. Future strategies to attract Chinese outbound tourism to Mexico

A number of practical suggestions come from this research work and can be used and be of interest mainly to national decision makers and national marketing departments.

Relevant market. Currently Mexico can receive tourists from all provinces, regions, municipalities and SARs, but it must concentrate on those with travel experience and which population is looking for exotic destinations. In terms of relevant market for Mexico there are about 200,000

Chinese tourists, according to outbound travel figures of 2007. This means 0.01% of the China's population, as depicted in the following figure.

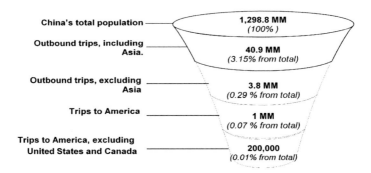

China's total population — 1,298.8 MM (100%)

Outbound trips, including Asia. — 40.9 MM (3.15% from total)

Outbound trips, excluding Asia — 3.8 MM (0.29 % from total)

Trips to America — 1 MM (0.07 % from total)

Trips to America, excluding United States and Canada — 200,000 (0.01% from total)

Fig. 6: Relevant market for Mexico, 2007[53]

The market opportunity is among those who have not travelled to Latin America yet, meaning those 3.6 million who went out of Asia, or mainly those 800,000 who visited the United States and Canada. This also includes those repeating a visit to the United States and who would like to link Mexico to complete their stay in America.

Target market. Different market segmentations have been done of the Chinese outbound market, by using the market structure developed by the Representation office of New York City in Shanghai[54]. Mexico will focus on the following two segments:

1. High-end tourism
Sophisticated groups select specific destinations. Mainly young professionals follow western travel patterns and are eager to set apart from the typical mass tourists. While in Mexico, this segment has stayed for a period of 10 to 12 days and spent around 7,000 to 22,000 USD per person

---

[53] Source: CNTA, 2008.
[54] Interview and information of the New York City tourism representation office in Shanghai, 26.02.2008.

for all services included (tours, accommodation, flight and meals).[55]. Main source regions are Beijing, Shanghai and Guangzhou.

2. Middle class tourism
Especially Meetings, Incentives, Conferences and Exhibitions (MICE) travel and segments which are known for travelling with a specific objective or event. They do not have such an extensive budget for personal expenses and hardly ask for stay extensions. Main source regions are Beijing, Shanghai, Guangzhou and capitals of the provinces.

3. Mass tourism
Mexico is far from being a mass tourism destination, mainly because this segment is quite sensitive to product prices. While travellers from this segment have strong Chinese characteristics and try to visit as many countries as they can in one single trip. When they are first-time travellers, they will choose Asiatic (similar culture and proximity) or European destinations (most countries represent an icon to them). Mass tourists come from all over China. Mexico should focus on the previously mentioned target groups and prepare to receive a limited number of massive tourists in the future. While products offered by market structure, the following characteristics must be considered regarding specific segments:

Segment	Offered products	Market participation	Spending power
Mass tourism	Famous cities "*Sightseeing*" All inclusive tours All year seasonality	Big volume Low profit margin Zero Fee risk	Low High price sensitivity
Middle class tourism	Moderate cultural exploration MICE Travel Tours during vacation in China	Medium volume Growth along with the middle class	Medium
High-end tourism	Thematic tours (Museums, art, ecological) Tailor made tours all year long	Low volume High growth	High Price is not relevant

Fig. 7: Tourism products by market structure, 2008[56]

---

[55] Interview with China Travel Mexico, 21.03.2008.
[56] Interview with the New York City tourism representation office in Shanghai, 26.02.2008.

Product adaptation and quality service

- Products have to be planned and adapted according to Chinese costumers' demands. Catering to Americans or Europeans is not the same as for Chinese.

- Signs and menus in the Chinese language will help to clearly establish the image of Mexico as a friendly destination to Chinese tourists. Some actions like the creation of a Chinatown in Mexico City's downtown are signs of the commitment of the country to China.

- Design a comprehensive strategy, which involves all industry towards the attraction of the Chinese market. Deliver quality services in terms of schedules, itineraries, products, fair prices, commissions and hospitality. Train the staff members in order to avoid misunderstandings regarding cultural differences, as well as competent Chinese speaking tourist guides.

- Familiarization tours (FAM tours) should by the synergic work of the government and the private sector (airlines, retailers, wholesalers, tourism associations and traders) should be constantly arranged.

- Educational seminars. Prepare the industry to understand the Chinese outbound market. In 2008, the author organized together with Mexico City's Tourism Board and COTRI (China Outbound Tourism Research Institute) the workshop "Strategies to attract Chinese tourists to Mexico". During the event, more than 60 participants gathered to discuss the current situation and future trends regarding the tourism product Mexico for international Chinese tourists.

Marketing

- Brand awareness of the product Mexico in China.

"From the viewpoint of consumerism, destinations and tourism products are perceived and evaluated as branded products, the construction of the imagined community of Chineseness results…" (Arlt 2006, 199).

What elements do we need to highlight while positioning Mexico as a brand? Mainly consider the cultural charms of Mexico. Let Chinese tourists get to know our cultural attractions and give the opportunity of comparing their civilization with the Mexican one. "They won't go to the beach because they still don't know the cultural Mexico" (Interview with a Shanghai tourism agent from China International Travel Services, CITS, 27.02.2008).

Support the Mexico brand with some highly estimated features by the Chinese tourists:

Mexico
Known as world heritage destinations, ancestral and cultural attractions, archaeology and architecture, a place where history and actuality merged, local handcrafts mixed with expensive shopping, wonderful Mexican cuisine, lots of entertainment, the door of China to Latin America, MICE destination, a safe place.

- The travel industry expressed the difficulty of selling Mexico as a principal/single destination. Therefore, Mexico will have to develop as the entry for Chinese tourists to South or North America. In that way, the tourists who have to travel for at least 20 hours can enjoy more than one destination. An example is Brazil as the hub in South America, some of the packages offered to Chinese tourists start with Brazil as the link to Peru and Argentina.
- Print materials, media, and Internet. Product information needs to be designed to target the high-end market. Special catalogues need to be available all year around, not just during fair participation or special gastronomic or educational events. Articles connected to destination attributes can be publish in enthusiast magazines and also industry related magazines or journals.

Concerning the media coverage, last November 2007, Jamaica and China celebrated 35 years of diplomatic relations. For this occasion, the China Central Television (CCTV) dedicated a whole week to promote Jamaica among its viewers. For seven days programs related to sports, tourism and culture were presented; those shows were previously recorded in Jamaica during the 2006 FAM trip organized by Jamaica's Embassy in China. Initiatives like this can be undertaken by Mexico with the support of the National Tourism Office established in Beijing, China.

Internet promotion is an effective and relatively cheap communication channel. A mixture of photos, product related information, blogs, and opinion forums gather in a single place and are translated into Chinese. CPTM (Consejo de Promoción Turística de Mexico) has adapted its platform in Chinese since 2007, but this still needs to be done by federal States and tourism related companies and organizations.

- Public Relations. Co-marketing activities between the Mexican tourism industry and important tour operators in China. The budget of this cooperation must be geared towards new product presentations, lectures of destination introduction and training for tour operators in China. Currently Mexico has a co-marketing agreement with China Youth Travel Service (CYTS) Beijing.

An effective way of meeting potential partners and clients is the participation in international tourism fairs and events. Mexico has already been in regional tourism fairs like Beijing International Travel & Tourism Market (BITTM) 2007, China International Travel Mart (CITM) 2007 and China Outbound Travel and Tourism Market (COTTM) 2008 and 2009.

5. Conclusion

Once the basic needs are covered, people intend to spend time and money on activities such as education and tourism. From the analysis of Chinese outbound tourism to Mexico, it must be recognized that attracting tourists is not the result of sporadic efforts or just the participation in international events, but is a solid commitment among government, private and academic institutions.

As a result of the research, the main constrains of Chinese outbound tourism to Mexico are: communication (written, spoken), limited flight connections and insufficient promotion of the destination. Mexico will be far from becoming a desirable destination for the Chinese if it cannot convey any clear images, mainly based on culture and history.

Communication goes beyond the simple signs in main touristic attractions, hotels or airports. It is about mutual understanding, little is known about both sides of the industry. By working together, the cultural gap can be narrowed which would result in easy to sell products and satisfied customers. On the other hand, training of human resources in hotels, restaurants and other service providers within the industry will generate "word of mouth" recommendations, allowing for the attraction of a larger number of tourists and the possibility of repeat visits to the destination.

Regarding flight connections, in spring 2008, the Mexican airline Aeromexico opened a direct flight from Mexico to Shanghai, which with a short layover in Tijuana, takes about 21 hours with a twice a week departure. This airline has become the first to connect China with Latin America, offering connections with Sao Paulo, Buenos Aires and Santiago de Chile. Unfortunately, due to H1N1 flu cases, Chinese government officials temporarily cancelled the direct flight in May after the confirmation of the first case of the flu in Asia, which was registered by a Mexican citizen staying in Hong Kong.[57] Mexican tourism stakeholders believe that the flights might be re-opened by March 2010.

Visa procedures continue being slow and difficult. By adopting the ADS scheme and promoting the group visa, the chance of losing potential tourists will decrease. Declarations from the INM mentioned that with technological adequacies and the help of authorized agencies and companies, improvements will be made to provide visa services to Bra-

---

[57] Milenio.com, 04.05.2009, http://www.milenio.com/node/208465.

zil, Russia, India and China.[58] During Mexico's participation in China COTTM 2009, the ambassador in Beijing Excellency Mr. Jorge Guajardo announced that by simplifying the visa process arrivals of Chinese visitors in Mexico can increase to 30 or 35 thousand by 2010. [59]

As has been pointed out in this article, Mexico possesses characteristics that will help to attract a significant number of Chinese outbound tourists despite the geographical distance between the two countries. In order to continue as an important tourism destination in Latin America and the world, it's economic, social and cultural advantages has to be considered to design a solid strategy towards the Chinese tourism market. These measures will be reflected in gross domestic product (GDP) growth, employment, investment and infrastructure development in the country.

---

[58] SECTUR (2009b), 03.07.2009,
http://www.sectur.gob.mx/wb/sectur/sect_Nuevas_politicas_de_visas_a_Mexico_promoviend.

[59] Excelsior, 24.04.09,
http://www.exonline.com.mx/diario/noticia/dinero/economia/mexico_presenta_oferta_turistica_en_feria_china/577887.

References

Arlt, Wolfgang G. (2006): *China's Outbound Tourism*. London/New York.

Blok, Anders (2002): *China Social Anthropology Study*. *Scandinavia Tourism Research report*, November. Tokyo (Scandinavian Tourist Board).

China Daily (2009): *China's GDP grows 7.9% in Q2*. 20.07.2009. http://www.chinadaily.com.cn/bizchina/2009-07/16/content_8435594.htm.

CNTA (2009): *National Tourism Working Conference opens in Beijing*, 08.01.2009. http://en.cnta.gov.cn/html/2009-1/2009-1-8-17-46-75892.html.

COTRI (2009): *China Outbound Tourism Quality Label Information*. 15.04.2009. http://www.china-outbound.com/index.php?option=com_content&view= article&id=73&Itemid=73.

CPTM (2008): *Analisis de Coyuntura, Temporada de Invierno 2008*. Mexico.

CYTS (2008): *China Youth Travel Service (CYTS) Catalogue*, Beijing.

Euromonitor Internacional (2007): *China: Country Market Insight October 2007*, London.

Excelsior (2009): *Mexico presenta oferta turística en feria china*. 24.04.09 http://www.exonline.com.mx/diario/noticia/dinero/economia/mexico_pres enta_oferta_turistica_en_feria_china/577887.

INEGI (2009): *Sistema de cuentas nacionales de Mexico. Cuenta Satelite de Turismo en Mexico, 2003 – 2006*. 20.02.2009. http://dgcnesyp.inegi.org.mx/cgi-win/bdiecoy.exe/739?c=12601.

Kim, Seongseop, Guo, Yingzhi, & Agrusa, Jerome (2005): Preference and positioning analyses of overseas destinations by Mainland Chinese outbound pleasure tourists. In: *Journal of Travel Research*, 44, 212–220.

Milenio.com (2009): *Suspende China vuelo directo con Mexico por influenza*. 04.05.2009. http://www.milenio.com/node/208465.

SECTUR (2009a): *Informes de Gobierno, apartados del sector turismo 2009*. Mexico.

SECTUR (2009b): *Nuevas politicas de visas a Mexico, promoviendo el turismo y la inversión*. 03.07.2009.http://www.sectur.gob.mx/wb/sectur/sect_Nuevas_politicas_de_ visas_a_Mexico_promoviend.

SECTUR (2009c): *Resultados de la actividad económica Enero – Diciembre 2008*. Mexico.

SECTUR (2008): *Desarrollo de Productos Turísticos*. 12.03.2009. http://www.sectur.gob.mx/wb/sectur/sect_Desarrollo_de_Productos_Turist icos.

SIMMT (2009): *SIMMT 2005 – 2008*. 22.07.2009. www.siimt.com.

Sparks, Beverly, Pan Grace Wen (2008): Chinese Outbound tourists: Understanding their attitudes, constraints and use of information sources. In: *Tourism Management* (2008), doi:10.1016/j.tourman. 2008.10.14.

SSAP (2007): *Chinese Tourism Research Annual 2006*, Beijing.

UNWTO (Hg.) (2000): *Tourism 2020 Vision Volume 3: East Asia and the Pacific*. Madrid.

UNWTO (Hg.) (2006): *China: The Asia and the Pacific Intra-Regional Outbound Series*. Madrid.

Marketing Jamaica to the Chinese outbound travel market

David L. Shields

It could be stated that the start of the tourism industry in the Caribbean, and in particular the Jamaican tourism industry, is attributed to the emergence of the steamboat industry. Since the 1840's steamers travelled from London to Kingston, and for many Europeans the trip to the West Indies was the fulfilment of a lifetime dream. So too for many Americans, Jamaica was on their radar and was now made accessible after a six day trip by these steamers.

Kingston, the Capital, was to play an important role in the 1870's, but with the development of the trade in bananas to North America this provided a new era in the tourism industry in Jamaica, both with the opening of new tourist areas within Jamaica the north coast) and this also acted as the catalysis for North American be become a new source market for Jamaica. Many national and international occurrences of the period began to impact the development of tourism to become an important activity in the economic life of the whole Jamaica. Moving from the south to the centre of the island, the impact of this burgeoning sector was to find a solid place in the north coast of the country. This region, with Montego Bay having a dedicated international airport, was soon to become the "tourist capital" of Jamaica. The impact of the tourism industry had now spread over the entire country of Jamaica.

With the now obvious role and importance of the industrial activity in Jamaica and the international interest being brought to the sector and to the destination, Jamaica, it was now important to have that important national framework and institution which would guide the development of the sector. The Tourist Trade Development Board was instituted with the responsibility for the development and promotion of Jamaica's tourist industry since 1922. After functioning for some years, that body had lost much of its relevance and in 1952 a recommendation from the International Bank for Reconstruction and Development for a board to include representatives from the industry was adopted and on April 1,

1955, the Jamaica Tourist Board (JTB) was established by Law 61 of 1954.

In 1955 visitor arrivals to Jamaica was reported to be 86,000 and increased to 227,000 in 1962, the year of Jamaica's independence from the United Kingdom. In 2008 stay over arrivals to Jamaica was 1,769,271, reflecting the growth over the years, not only in the number of visitors, but also growth in the overall size and impact of the tourism industry and the ability of the destination to welcoming these persons to the shores of the Island. The industry today, while being somewhat heavily dependent on the US market for majority of its visitors, has diversified and shows Canada and the United Kingdom as the second and third largest markets, respectively. The share of arrivals to Jamaica for the full year 2008 shows the United States having a 65.1% share, Canada 13.4% and the United Kingdom 10.7%. Europe, Asia and the Caribbean have also shown growth in arrivals and increases in market share of the years, thus facilitating the mandate of the Tourism Master Plan for Sustainable Development, to diversify the market risk and dependence on any one market, and at the same time, growing latent markets and building an appropriate airlift strategy to sustain the growth.

The Jamaica Tourist Board (JTB) has been at the leadership of the promotion and marketing of Jamaica as the "premier warm weather Caribbean destination" and its efforts continue to be global in coverage. With its headquarters in Kingston, Jamaica, the JTB delivers high quality marketing and sales presentations to travel trade and consumers through a network of staff personnel and agency representation in all of the major source markets. The United States, representing some 65% of arrivals has its main office in Miami, Florida and this facility serves the United States through a satellite office in New York and staff operating from home-bases across the country.

In Toronto, the JTB operates from the same facility as the Offices of the Jamaican Consul General in Toronto, and uses a similar model for field service as that of the United States, where personnel operate from home bases and cover the market. Most of the Canadian representatives are however located in the main office in Toronto. The London office serves the United Kingdom with all personnel working from a central location in central London.

In Eastern Europe that market is managed from the Jamaican Embassy in Berlin, Germany where a JTB Regional Director is based, with responsibility for all the markets and managing the various contracted representatives, based in the respective European markets, to service the needs of the travel community and engage in a number of consumer promotions. The markets of Latin America are managed by an independent representative whose activities are coordinated through the Miami office, while the representatives of China, India and Japan are managed through the Headquarters in Kingston, Jamaica.

With this infrastructure and the commitment of the Government of Jamaica to supporting the efforts of tourism development and promotions, Jamaica continues to see growth in the stay over visitor arrivals. To the end of August 2009, Jamaica welcomed some 1,319,704 stay over visitors, representing a 3.1% growth. Only two countries within the Caribbean reported growth in the arrivals, based on Caribbean Tourism Organisation (CTO) data to August, Cuba and Jamaica. Considering the global market conditions, this is quite an accomplishment and shows the confidence the marketplace has in the destination, and is in part due to the efforts at encouraging new investments in tourism infrastructure this sector and also to significant improvements in the overall tourism support infrastructure.

China/Jamaica Relationship

In February 2005 Jamaica played host to the First China-Caribbean Economic & Trade Cooperation Forum held in the capital city, Kingston. The event signalled a most significant move by some the Caribbean Community, CARICOM, and the Government of the People's Republic of China. CARICOM, the Caribbean Community, is an organisation of 15 Caribbean nations and dependencies, and some members, including Jamaica, have maintained long and positive political and trade relations with China.

For Jamaica's important tourism industry the most important outcome of the Forum was the February 2005 signing of the Memorandum of Understanding between the Government of the People's Republic of China and the Ministry of Tourism of Jamaica for the "promotion of group travel." The MOU states that both sides: "Have agreed on the facilitation of group travel by Chinese tourist to Jamaica".

Jamaica has always had strong positive diplomatic relations with China and has articulated the "One China" policy in diplomatic relations. Diplomatic relations were first established in 1972, but from as far back as

1854 the first 472 Chinese arrives into Jamaica. Today, Chinese visitors to Jamaica travel both for business and leisure and reflect the current profile of Chinese travellers, many of whom are affluent and sophisticated travellers exploring the world.

For some observers, 2005 marked an interesting time in the process of managing tourism activities under the arrangements for Approved Destination Status (ADS), and Jamaica sought first to understand the opportunities and challenges of the system and to determine those Chinese trade partners who would be critical to the growth of the travel to the Caribbean, and to Jamaica in particular. It was important that at the outset to identify the key Jamaican Ministries and Agencies which would collaborate on the implementation of the ADS and in executing those activities to attract the Chinese tourist to Jamaica.

With the establishment of the Embassy of Jamaica in Beijing on the 15th July 2005, Jamaica now had an operating base in China and a critical centre for the development of the ADS and tourism in China. The most critical step was to confirm those tour operators from the Chinese side with whom the Jamaica Tourist Board would be working, as well as from the Jamaica side, to confirm with the CNTA the list of Jamaican operators who would be active in the Chinese market effort. The engagement was sought from the Ministry of National Security (Immigration Department) and the Ministry of Foreign Affairs and Foreign Trade (Embassy of Jamaica in Beijing), working closely with the Jamaica Tourist Board and our representative agency, China Business Network (CBN) to implement a multi-segment market approach to attracting the Chinese to Jamaica. CBN was appointed in 2005 to assist with the initial steps to reaching this market.

The Process
Immediately after signing the Memorandum of Understanding with the CNTA, the marketing agency for the Ministry of Tourism, the Jamaica Tourist Board (JTB) sent a delegation to Beijing to participate in the first staging of the Beijing Travel & Tourism Market (BITTM) in April 2005. This first effort was supported by members of the private sector, including Destination Management Companies (DMC) and hoteliers who sought to explore the possibilities for business. Among these were Glamour Tours, Caribic Vacations, SuperClubs and Half Moon Resort. This was primarily an exploratory market visit and proved extremely use-

ful for the delegation in understanding many of the nuisances of the market, mainly on questions of the procedure for issuing visas for travel, knowledge of the location of the destination, availability of Chinese food and language guides.

Through a series of seminars, the JTB's management prepared briefing documents on the requirements of the Chinese travel trade and immediately moved to implementation of a regime for management of the process for "group travel". The Embassy of Jamaica in Beijing was to play the most critical role in order to ensure compliance with the MOU signed in February 2005. Both the CNTA and the MOT shared the list of "approved" Tour Operators and work began to fine tune the visa issuing protocol. It was agreed that only a limited number of Tour Operators would be considered for collaboration in the first instance, with the minimum requirement being that of knowledge of the destination and an active programme for development of the Chinese outbound market.

To ensure a full understanding of the travel trade and the key indicators for building awareness of Jamaica, as well as expanding the desire for travel to Jamaica among the targeted Chinese consumers, it was important to have a partner who could guide the JTB through this process. After discussions in Beijing and follow up talks in London with Dr. Adam Wu of China Business Network (CBN), is was agreed that this organization would represent the interest of Jamaica in our efforts at understanding the Chinese travel market and support the efforts at building the Chinese outbound tourism market to Jamaica. In large part, the increased presence of Jamaica in the Chinese travel trade in as a result of the professional guidance of CBN, and the commitment and support of the Board of Director of the JTB.

Among the first activities of the new partnership with CBN was that of assessing the trade relations and determining the best opportunities for achieving the quickest return, and to agree on the targeted niche and then determine programmes in support of reaching the primary audience. Numerous trade activities were planned supported by media and promotional events which would selectively aid the overall efforts. The newly established Embassy of Jamaica in China was a critical partner at every step in the process providing guidance and ensuring collaboration with other Chinese-based stakeholders.

Understanding the Chinese Travel Market

The most important thing to do in early 2005, as we looked at the large population of over 1.3 billion people, is to determine a strategic approach to be taken to approach the market. It was immediately agreed that the approach would seek to determine the following:

- Identify and verify qualification of the travel trade partners important for the selling of Jamaica from the list provided by the CNTA.
- Implement a programme of engagement of these persons which would include educational seminars and fam trips.
- Determine the geographic market areas to be targeted and the approach to be made and the support to be given to growing these areas.
- Agree on the overall positing of Jamaica, the market segment to be communicated to and the brand promise to be offered.
- Identify collaborative efforts with other state agencies which would provide synergistic value to Jamaica, these would include the Ministry of National Security (Immigration) and the Ministry of foreign Affairs and Foreign Trade.
- Identify the destination management organisations in Jamaica which would be able to quickly provide the language and local tourism support in Jamaica for Chinese groups.

With a long history of association of the Chinese-Jamaican community with the broader Jamaican community, there was the need to review the existing perceptions among the tourism partners and the community in general, to determine the response to efforts at building this market, and determine how the industry would react to efforts at attracting Chinese visitors to our resorts and attractions. Growth in overall commercial activities, including retail trade with China, as well as the active participation of the Chinese in infrastructure development has helped to create a very positive feeling about the potential of a growing Chinese visitor market to Jamaica. Work with the University of the West Indies (UWI) and the local Chinese Benevolent Association also helped to create a very positive feeling about the Chinese community in Jamaica and a more welcoming environment for visitors.

It became very clear in our early review of the opportunities for the generation of business from the Chinese market to Jamaica that we needed to have very successful alliance with local organizations. This was important as it was determined that this would provide critical support in assisting the JTB's effort in having the tourism entities and businesses adapt their products, to respond to the cultural nuances of the Chinese. This is not dissimilar to the approach which was taken in attracting the Japanese tourist to Jamaica in the 1980's. Advertising and participation in trade show needed to be supported by the development of specialized packages for the general leisure group tourist under the ADS agreement, as well as the increasing number of business visitor (with interest in tourism sites and accommodation) and the smaller numbers, but growing affluent segment of self-organised sophisticated travellers, interested in Jamaica. Engagement of the local tourism sector was most important and this was done through presentations and active engagement of the Jamaica Hotel & Tourist Association (JHTA).

Marketing

In the development and implementation of the marketing plan for Jamaica in the Chinese market, it was quickly agreed that what was needed was an approach to the market recognizing the peculiarity of the culture as well as the challenges of distance and limited air access. We reviewed our objectives for the market and summarized these as follows: the marketing and sales activities of JTB in China is to develop and market Jamaica to the outbound travel trade, as well as to the sophisticated travelling public so that JAMAICA remains the premier Caribbean destination for Chinese visitors coming to invest, to do business, as well as to enjoy high quality leisure activities for incentive travel and holidaying.

We therefore sought to identify some key elements of the marketing which would guide the activities in China which are the following.

Participation in the Chinese Tourist Welcoming Award

An efficient way to communicate the special focus of Jamaica on the Chinese market is the participation in the CTW Chinese Tourists Welcoming Award. The CTW Award is held annually since 2004 to collect and distribute knowledge and best practice examples from tourism destinations and companies working in the field. During COTTM in 2008, Jamaica was awarded with the CTW Chinese Tourists Welcoming Award on the category Media/Internet, honour personally accepted by the Hon. Tourism Minister of Jamaica, Edmund Bartlett. In 2009 Jamaica received a GOLD award in the category of Service Quality, another indication of the successful implementation of targeted programmes against the sophisticated Chinese travelling market. This activity, while allowing Jamaica to be recognised among some of the leading outbound tourism players in the Chinese market, also provided an opportunity to benchmark the activities of Jamaica against those of major, more developed tourism destinations, some of whom had greater access to the Chinese market.

In 2008 Hon. Minister Bartlett while attending the COTTM in Beijing highlighted the fact that Jamaica was among the first countries in the Caribbean establishing diplomatic relationships with China and Jamaica has been welcoming Chinese delegations of officials, investors, business executives and leisure travellers since ADS agreement taking effect in the middle of 2005. Accompanied by the Director General of Tourism, the Director of Tourism (JTB) and Dept. Director of Tourism (JTB), Minister Bartlett received the Chinese Tourists Welcome Award on behalf of Jamaica Tourism Board for its innovative marketing approach in China.

Website

The Jamaica Tourism Board commissioned the China Business Network in 2005 to develop its Chinese web site www.visitjamaica.com.cn with the purpose of raising the awareness of Jamaica among the travel trade as well as would be travellers throughout China. It was important also that the presentation of Jamaica was not only in the overall look and feel of the site but to ensure that the content was adapted to the Chinese taste and styles using this medium.

The Chinese web site of JTB has been among the most popular web pages on the award winning World Travel Online on the China Wide Web with over 300,000 page views each month and on average 50,000 Unique User Sessions per month. Not surprisingly, Jamaica Tourism Board received Gold Award for the effective online marketing and offline promotional activities in China.

Traditional tourism destination can be found in guidebooks and other sources of information available in Chinese bookshops; Chinese glossy travel magazines and so on. With little knowledge and awareness of Jamaica there was remains very little available information on the destination, especially prior to the Beijing Olympics in 2008. Working with media entities and writers (visiting journalists) the intention is to expand Jamaica's presence in guidebooks and resources in an effort to broaden the reach and awareness of the destination. Jamaica has since 2005 upgraded its Chinese web site and now employs version 2 at www.visitjamaica.com.cn

The use of e-marketing extends beyond the destination web site to the use of other travel related sites which communicated the work of the JTB and the activities being developed to engage the travel community in China. CBN would utilize the web sites in China to release news about visits to China to the relevant members of China Travel and Tourism Club (www.lvyou168.cn/CTTC) and identified those most interested in Jamaica and invited the key decision makers of the most important outbound tour operators and corporate travel organizers in both Shanghai and Beijing to meet up with the delegation either during the exhibitions being attended or for their participation in evening receptions.

Trade Fairs

Since 2005, Jamaica has participated in regional tourism fairs like World Travel Fair 2008 (in Shanghai), China International Travel Market 2007 (Kunming) and COTTM China Outbound Travel and Tourism Mart (Beijing), at the inaugural staging of the Beijing International Travel & Tourism Market (BITTM) in 2005.

With the participation of some Jamaican private sector entities, the destination has been able to present itself as the foremost Caribbean destination active with the Chinese travel trade. Among the entities which have participated are the high end luxury resort brands, the all-inclusive properties and a number of Destination Management Organisations (DM Companies). The inclusion of the private sector is critical to the work of the JTB in China as they play an important role in the verification of the group travel itinerary and are an important aspect of the visa issuing procedure.

With the engagement of China Business Network (CBN) among the travel trade clients from Jamaica to follow up those interested Chinese tour operators from the exhibitions and to promote their services further and by developing and maintaining their Chinese web pages. The web strategy here was one of the early initiatives in order to provide a central location for information on the marketing efforts to the Jamaican trade partners with links back to their individual business web sites. The web strategy assisted in building a mini-database which included all those companies and travel professionals that showed interests in sending visitors to Jamaica, thereby building a community of trade partners and media entities with interest in Jamaica.

Top End consumer promotions
To satisfy the increasing interests generated by the promotional activities both online and offline and to raise the profile of Jamaica as the premier destination in the Caribbean, Hon. Minister Bartlett (Minister of Tourism for Jamaica) led a delegation of senior officials from both Jamaican Ministry of Tourism and JTB to China in April 2008 to support the "Jamaica in China Week" organized by the Embassy of Jamaica in China in collaboration with the Ritz Carlton Financial Centre Hotel. The partnership of both Jamaica Tourist Board (JTB) and the Ritz Carlton was deemed an important strategy to assist in the positioning of Jamaica with an International luxury brand and to promote that connection in China. The Ritz Carlton Rose Hall Montego Bay was also involved with this effort through the use of Jamaican chefs to promote the food of Jamaica. Reggae music played an important role in presenting aspects of Jamaica's musical heritage to an upscale Chinese audience as well as a presentation on the variety of interesting Jamaican foods.

The Jamaica week was further enhanced by Jamaica's participation in the COTTM i.e. China Outbound Travel and Tourism market from April 14th to 16th, 2008. Minister Bartlett was invited as the Guest of Honour and gave a keynote speech during the opening ceremony.

Collateral
Review of the full range of collateral which could be adapted for use in China and translation of these into Mandarin, while retaining the positioning for the destination. In the development of the promotional materials great care was taken to communicate a relevant positioning of Jamaica within China, while being able to retain and be consistent with the global positioning of "Once You Go, You Know". The collaterals were translated (wherever necessary), new materials developed and important elements considered in order to present the sophistication of the destination to the Chinese marketplace.

Strategic Trade Relations

A multi-pronged approach was used in the development of the Chinese market for Jamaica. While efforts were being made to ensure a solid trade based to ensure commercial activities and targeted consumer activities, the JTB engaged with the Embassy of Jamaica in China, an approach which saw senior officials of the Government of Jamaica engaging with key Chinese state agencies to ensure development and sustainability of the travel distribution channel. Such meetings included the China National Tourism Administration (CNTA) as well as the China Civil Aviation Administration.

Consumer Trade Shows & Seminars

The various trade and consumers shows were conducted in the key geographic areas of Beijing and Shanghai with a view to capturing the attention of the lucrative, affluent and sophisticated audience in these areas. China Business Network provided Jamaica Tourist Board with complete solution in assisting visiting Jamaican delegation to reap the most benefits of attending the exhibitions. Service provided by the local China based organization, CBN included, but not limited to:

- Negotiating with the exhibition organizers to book the best available booth at the most cost effective way i.e. sharing the stands with CBN as to receive continuous supports from CBN's multilingual staff
- Creatively designing and printing booth banners, posters, collaterals as well as business cards in Chinese for the participates of Jamaica delegation
- Arranging the most influential news media to interview the Ambassador of Jamaica to China and Deputy Director of Jamaica Tourist Boards, ensuring many news releases and length reports of the Jamaican delegation and the country as a top tourism destination
- Inviting many Chinese outbound tour operators and corporate travel organizers coming to meet up with the Jamaican delegation and facilitating many trade professionals in talking with the Jamaica delegates during the two exhibitions.

Special Event Opportunities

- **Beijing Olympics 2008**

  2008 proved the year of Jamaica in China with Jamaica's tremendous success during the Beijing Olympics.

  The Hon. Edmund Bartlett, Minister for Tourism and Ms. Olivia "Babsy" Grange, Minister of Information, Culture, Youth and Sport visited Beijing to witness and celebrate Jamaica's achievements.

  Chinese outbound tour operators were very impressed by the straight forward visa procedure and much practical supports provided by Jamaican Embassy in Beijing and also the increased accessibility by air travel via USA, Mexico and also by Air Jamaica from European destination to Jamaica. Now, this amazing place has been granted the name of "the home country of the world fastest man and world records maker". In answering the question how Jamaica produced such fine athletes Minister Bartlett humorously said "Once You Go, You Know".

- **China International Fair for Investment and Trade (CIFIT) 2007**

  In collaboration with other state Agencies, the JTB has aggressively employed a collaborative strategy which seen the organization working with the Jamaican trade and investment promotions agency as well as major Jamaican export organizations, such as the Coffee Industry agency to promote Jamaica and Jamaica's tourism to this market. In 2007 Jamaica's participation in the China International Fair for Investment and Trade saw the JTB having a major role in the City of Xiamen, host venue for the Fair. There the JTB presented elements of the destination such as the location, the infrastructure, the food and the first class facilities available both for investors and for visitors.

Media Relations and coverage

Another efficient way of marketing is the production of TV series which present information about Jamaica as a travel destination. In November 2007, Jamaica and China celebrated 35 years of diplomatic relations, in that matter China Central Television (CCTV) dedicated an entire week to promote Jamaica's best touristic, cultural and sports attractions.

The efforts on CBN and the Jamaica Tourist Board, in collaboration with the Embassy of Jamaica in China were geared at maximizing the exposure and effects of the Jamaican delegation two major PR events were organized with additional objectives.

The first one was in Tong Mao Hotel where the owners of real Blue Mountain Coffee established the first Jamaican coffee outlet and shop in China. The event was to officially open the coffee outlet while use the opportunity to promote tourism and travel to Jamaica. This presented a big breakthrough for Jamaica in Shanghai.

The second event was organized in Beijing Kerry Centre where the Ambassador of Jamaica to China played host to other foreign dignitaries and invited travel professionals. The event was used to officially launch the first version of the Chinese web site for Jamaica Tourist Board (www.visitjamaica.com.cn).

Real blue mountain coffee and Jamaican Rum were provided for Chinese to taste real the Jamaica, as well as well presented authentic Jamaican food including jerk chicken, Jamaican meat patties and Jamaican desserts. The events were accompanied by Jamaican performers who entertained the invited guests and Jamaica delegation and gave Chinese travel professionals the real flavour of Jamaica as a land of music and dance. Invited travel trade professionals were able to engage in business discussion with trade delegates from Jamaica.

Chinese main media including CCTV and travel trade press were present to report the events hence, to increase the promotion of Jamaica further throughout China.

Fam Trip

For the Tourism Outlook Seminar of 2009, the Jamaican authorities invited a FAM Tour composed of Tour operators and Media representatives from China, including also the celebrity rock star Mr. Cui Jian. Both groups will have meetings with tourism main stakeholders and will experience the destination by first-hand, in order to strength travel business relations. The communications theme of Jamaica is "Once You Go, You Know" and this is especially true for members of the travel trade. Encouraging travel partners to see the destination is one of the deliverables for success as it in this experience that travel professionals and media can truly determine the fit of Jamaica to their clients and ensure the effective selling to the marketplace.

Based on results from the 2009 trade and media trip the activity was a success as reports carried were immediately online without time delay by the World Travel Online and CCTV web editor; such reports were enhanced by a series of TV program that was released within one month after the Fam trip returned to China. A half hour long feature program on Jamaica followed with daily broadcasting of "On the Road" program with every day featuring one aspect of Jamaica for 5 days within a week. These programs were repeated on the Travel Channel in China.

In 2006 the JTB hosted the China Central Television (CCTV 9), the English Channel to Jamaica for a feature in the "Travelog" programme. This programme has since been aired on numerous occasions and continues to reinforce the many positive attributes of the destination, which are of importance to the sophisticated Chinese audience.

Next Stage of Marketing

With the positioning to the more affluent, sophisticated Chinese travellers, Jamaica is set to separate from the broad focus being given to mass traffic from China. The current attention from the high end Chinese tour operators, the interest of the travel trade as well as the support being received from private sector stakeholders in the destination, it is important that Jamaica should and will continue the focus on the quality aspects and attributes of the destination. The demonstration of this commitment could see Jamaica becoming the destination of quality and distinction in the Caribbean for the Chinese, a position which will work to Jamaica's advantage, as we turn the disadvantage of geographical distance, into an advantage. The implementation of this effort combined with an arrangement to facilitate easy, same-day travel to Jamaica, even where this might include multiple stops, would be an important development in support of the positioning strategy.

Along with the leadership from the Ministry of Tourism and Jamaica Tourist Board, China can become an even more important source market for Jamaica.

References

Arlt, Wolfgang Georg: Director, COTRI China Outbound Tourism Research Institute, *China as a new tourism source market for Jamaica.*

Caribbean Community (CARICOM) Secretariat : *Revised Treaty of Chaguaramas establishing the Caribbean Community, including the CRICOM Single Market & Economy.*

China Business Network, Market Assessment Report.

Shields, David L.: *Jamaica Hotel & Tourist Association, Annual General Meeting (AGM) Presentation, "Jamaica: Marketing to the Chinese".*

Beyond "Chocolate and Brussels"?
An exploratory analysis of cross cultural perception and travel experience of Chinese student tourists in Flemish cities

Zhang Yang & Pang Ching Lin

1. Mapping the context

In the imagination of most Chinese Belgium represents a small country, located in remote Western Europe. Its 30,278 square kilometres land has almost the same (small) size of Taiwan Island. It seems fair to state that it does not rank high among the most favourite European destinations for potential Chinese tourists.

As of 2004 when the tourism agreement of ADS (Approved Destination Status) between the European Union and the China National Tourism Administration (CNTA) was signed, European travel package of Chinese tourists has become very popular (Arlt & Freyer 2008). Belgium is part of this package tour. However, it does not represent a strong attraction for Chinese tourist groups. Given the high price Chinese tourists pay for an European tour, they aspire to see as many countries as possible (Wagner 2007). Most tours are arranged in patterns like "11 countries in 14 days". Therefore, visits to small and "less well known" countries are limited in time. Most Chinese have minimal knowledge about Belgium except for "chocolates and Brussels". It should not come as a surprise that Flanders, the northern region in Belgium, is even less known in China. Nevertheless, there has been a steady increase of Chinese tourists to Belgium, especially in Brussels and Flanders in the past five years. Among the cities, Brussels, Antwerp and Leuven have attracted relatively high numbers of Chinese tourists.

In the current Chinese package tours to Europe in accordance with the ADS agreement, a visit to Brussels entails only half a day. And most Chinese guests stay just for one night in Brussels because of low accommodation prices. In sum, Belgium stands for a short visit to the Grand Place/Grote Markt, the Atomium and Manneken Pis for Chinese travellers. Most do not even remember the names of these spots. Notwithstanding the efforts of Flemish government to promote more indepth tourism in Flanders by setting up a Flemish Tourism Office in Beijing in 2005, this initiative has not been able to change the current arrangement of half a day visit to Brussels. Therefore, most Chinese group tourists do not have the possibility to explore Flemish cities.

However, a growing number of Chinese students find their way to Belgian universities in recent years. The increase is especially noticeable in the largest university of the country, namely the University of Leuven. During their study period, most students seize the opportunity to travel as an integral part of the overall overseas study experience. Given the many constraints they face financially, administratively and time-wise-they mostly make city trips within the country. In addition, because of their intellectual background they develop an interest for the history, customs and culture of Flanders. Therefore, Chinese students in Belgium constitute the main Chinese visitors of Flemish cities.

The Flemish Tourism Office promotes on its website five main cities in Flanders: Antwerp, Ghent, Bruges, Mechelen, and Leuven. Yet Chinese students also visit Brussels as the capital of Belgium and Europe. This exploratory article is based on participant observation and informal conversations of the Chinese student-researcher travelling with her fellow Chinese friends in the cities of Antwerp, Brussels, Ghent and Bruges, followed by an in-depth interview with each Chinese student individually after each city trip.

2. Theoretical approaches

Perception is the process through which people see and make sense of the world around them (Schiffman and Kanuk 1987). To be more precise, perception is a "process by which an individual selects, organizes, and interprets stimuli into a meaningful and coherent picture of the world" (Schiffman and Kanuk 1987: 174). Perception is the result of a number of interrelated external and internal environmental factors. In the literature, the intricate relationship between culture, social interaction and perception is often noted. Perception is shaped by culture (Samovar and Porter 1991). The world and thus cultures have become more interconnected since globalization. Culture, according to Hannerz (2002) is a global process based on the organization of differences. He furthermore places tourism and migration in the context of globalization arguing that the two are interrelated phenomena. They both serve as critical mediums in shaping, visualizing and structuring cultural diversity. Besides other things, globalization has made cultural nobilities increasingly salient, thus rendering intercultural communication and encounters (Nesbitt 2004) even more complex, multi-layered and thus an intellectual challenge to grasp and to make sense of. By cultural mobilities, we refer to the mobilities of people and of ideas, images and commodities. Besides the mobilities, there is the speed of the flows, often facilitated by the media such as advertising (Gartner and Hunt 1987), travel agents (Perry 1978), travel brochures (Phelps 1986) and internet applications. In addition, the shift from production to consumption in the late capitalist society also needs to be taken into account when studying perception and intercultural encounters in general (Appadurai 1986; Bourdieu 1984; Featherstone 1991; Ferguson 1990) and in relation to contemporary China (Latham 2006; Link, Madsen & Pickowicz 2002; Liu 2004; Wu & Murphy 1994). Perceptions and meanings are dynamic cultural constructs. People differ in their perceptions because they have different views of the world (Krech & Crutchfield 1948; Robertson 1970; Nesbitt 2004). As a result, perceptions as open-ended and dynamic processes can be re-invented, re-assembled and consciously or unconsciously manipulated. Perceptions can distorted by biased sources of information, culturally influenced media, stereotypes, ethnocentrism, physical appearance and a quick jumping to a conclusion, the so-called "halo effect". Distorted perception can be also redressed by a plural representation of cultures and preferences through advertising, personal communication, persuasion or perception checking (Gudykunst and Kim, 1997).

Pre-perception, an important part of perception is shaped by a wide range of external and internal factors. It is an interesting exercise to compare pre- and post-travel perceptions in order to better understand the dynamics of perception making among tourists. Many researchers insist on the differences between tourist pre-travel and post-travel experiences (Pearce, 1980; Reisinger, 1990). Yet this is contested by Yum (1988), arguing that the travel experience does not produce changes in post-travel perceptions. Tourists can modify their perceptions of the host country (Pearce, 1982) in negative and in positive ways. This view suggests that pre- and post-perceptions are similar and the apparent changes in post-travel perceptions are not significant. For example, Pizam et al., (1991) found out that the travel experience did not change the attitude of US students towards the USSR and the Soviet people. This seems to apply to Chinese student tourists' pre-perception to Belgium and Flanders.

3. Exploring Some Specific Characteristics of Chinese Tourists' Perception and Travel Experience

The opportunity for Chinese to travel outside Mainland China for leisure is a new practice. However, Chinese in the middle and top incomes are already starting to consider travel a 'birthright'. The number of Chinese taking outbound trips continues to grow (CNTA, 2006). There is general agreement that the rapid development of China's economy is leading to a concomitant increase in international travel from a burgeoning middle class. The Chinese Government loosened the restriction on the outbound tourism market in 1983 when Chinese mainland residents could visit relatives in Hong Kong. ADS is an agreement between China and another country or group of countries regulating the issuing of visa to group travellers. This type of travel is usually an all-inclusive package tour. The number of ADS countries continues to expand for Chinese outbound tourists. By the end of February 2009, the Chinese government had granted ADS to 137 countries, including the United States and Taiwan (Xinhua, 2009). China has been identified as one of two major emerging outbound tourism markets in the world. In 2007, some 41 million Chinese engaged in outbound travel (CNTA, 2008). There has been a growing interest in researching outbound Chinese tourists (Arlt, 2006; Yu& Weiler, 2001).

For Belgium, according to the statistic of Flanders Tourism Office and Wallonia Tourism Office, only 14,667 Chinese people visited Belgium in 1993. Ten years later, the number climbed to 134,592 in 2003. It seems that more and more Chinese tourists travel to Belgium from the Belgian perspective. Nevertheless, Belgium only shared 2.01% of the total Chinese market in this year. In 2004, along with the signature of the agreement of ADS between European Union and Chinese government, Belgium and other 27 European countries became the destinations for Chinese group tourists. In 2004, 145,548 Chinese tourists visited Belgium, an increase of 8% compared to 2003. So far, the number of Chinese visitor was never less than 140,000.

As regards the experience of Chinese tourists in visiting the historical cities in Belgium, they lack insights to enable them to enjoy these cities. The trend of Chinese tourists' visit is on the decline. Fortunately, this decreasing trend is rather small. In 2002, 121,743 Chinese tourists travelled to Belgian historical cities.

Fig. 1: Development of Chinese tourists in Belgium[60]

However, the number has fallen to 93,754 in 2007. According to the statistics of Flanders Tourism Office, the historical cities in Belgium are Antwerp, Bruges, Brussels, Ghent, Leuven and Mechelen. Leuven is not the subject of this article but it would be helpful to include it in the statistics. Although the market share is dominated by Antwerp and other cities, Brussels remains the most attractive city for Chinese tourists. In 2007, it still received 72,306 Chinese tourists. Antwerp and Bruges kept growing since 2003, reaching 17.63% of the total in 2007. However, after a short increase in 2004, the market share of Ghent, Leuven and Mechelen has been constantly decreased.

Chinese student tourists constitute just one part of Chinese outbound tourists. It remains to be seen whether the travel experience of Chinese students correspond partially or entirely with Chinese outbound group tourists. As to motivations and behaviour of Chinese outbound travellers, it is instructive to look at the work of Arlt and Freyer (2006). At present, most of Chinese outbound tourists to Europe are organized. In this respect, student travellers form the exception to this general rule.

---

[60] The statistic of Belgium Tourism, Flanders Tourism Office,1994-2008.

103

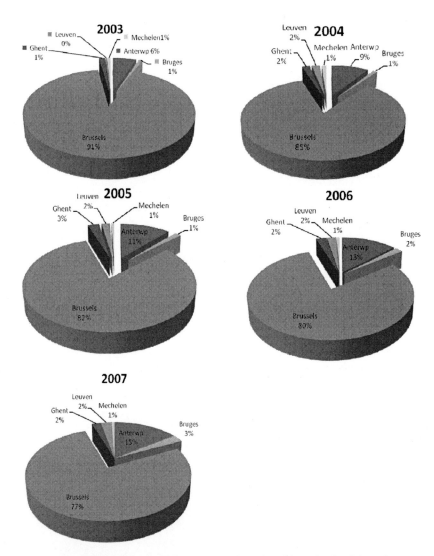

Fig. 2: Distribution of Chinese tourists in historical cities from 2003 to 2007[61]

---

[61] The statistic of Belgium Tourism, Flanders Tourism Office, 1994-2008.

Chinese travellers differ in many ways from Western tourists. Chinese mass-tourists do not seem to be interested in the conventional holiday products: 3S-holidays for mass tourists, cultural or nature-oriented tourism. Relaxation and fun, central to Western travellers, are not the main motivations for travel for the Chinese. Instead it is "more of an educational tour — practically a research trip or expedition their goal is to absorb as much as possible, about these peculiar Europeans" (Wagner 2007:2). International travel is a nascent practice, only accessible to those who can afford it. They are interested in seeing as many countries as possible and the most famous landmarks of each of them. Comparison with China especially with regard to modernity and state-of-the-art technology and architecture is always on the mind of Chinese travellers. Given the full program of visiting many countries in a short time, they do not have the time or the ambition to immerse in local cultures. Even more since, they prefer to travel in groups and rely on tour guides and translators to provide them information. Shopping is often valued higher than sightseeing in contrast to Western package tour travellers. Chinese outbound tourists prefer to spend considerable time on shopping for suitable gifts for important personalities at home than doing more sightseeing. Photographic documentation is almost even important as hunting for brand-name items. These pictures serve as show-and-exhibit for the people at home.

Concerning the travel behaviour of the Chinese students, they do share some of the general characteristics of Chinese mass tourists. Yet they also differ in some ways.

4. Methodology

Participant observation is a research method that aims to gain a close and intimate familiarity with a given group of individuals (such as a religious, occupational, or subcultural group, or a particular community) and their practices through an intensive involvement with people in their cultural environment, often though not always over an extended period of time. The method originated in field work of social anthropologists, especially Bronisław Malinowski and his students in Britain, the students of Franz Boas in the US, and in the urban research of the Chicago School of Sociology. It is part of ethnographic fieldwork, which involves a wide range of methods: informal interviews, direct observations, participation in the life of the group, collective discussions, analysis of personal documents produced within the group, self-analysis, and life-histories. Although the method is generally characterized as qualitative research, it can (and often does) include quantitative dimensions. It emerged as the principal approach to ethnographic research by anthropologists and relied on the cultivation of personal relationships with local informants as a way of learning about a culture, involving both observing and participating in the social life of a group. To sum up, there are three positive aspects of participant observation. First, it attempts to represent the voices and the views of the informants themselves. Second, it seeks to understand action: as to how and why practices and relations change. The last but the most important is that the fieldworker transforms the field notes and findings into a scientifically grounded ethnographic account.

In order to assess the perception and the experience of Chinese student tourists in Flemish cities, participant observation and in-depth interviews are employed. The research subjects are four Chinese friends of the researcher. These four students originate from different provinces of China but have obtained the same scholarship from Chinese government to study in K.U.Leuven as joint- promotion PhD student or PhD candidate. They arrived at about the same period and stay for a similar period of study time. This shared background also explains why they have become travel mates. Because of legal-administrative constraints as foreigners, they cannot travel outside the country. From September to November 2008, they made daytrips to the cities of Brussels, Antwerp, Bruges and Ghent. They also visited the university town Leuven, where they study. These daytrips are not planned beforehand but rather an ad hoc decision during their MSN discussion in their free time. Although Mechelen is promoted by the Tourism Office of Flanders as a historical town, none of them felt compelled to visit it.

The author participated in all their trips to these cities. Prior to the trip, she has devised the following outline of observations and interviews as follows:

- Convenience of independent travel
- Mode of Transportation
- Gathering travel information
- Language barrier

- Quality of tourism guidebook (especially the guidebook in Chinese)
- The perception of the Flemish cities
- The perception of cultural and historical buildings and area (including museums, churches and towers, city halls, Chinatowns, Grand places, castles, monasteries)
- The perception of modern buildings and other destinations
- The perception of the natural landscape
- The perception of souvenir
- The perception of local people
- The general impression of a city

The researcher interacted with the student tourists in a spontaneous, informal way. She did not present the above questions directly to the Chinese student travellers. Instead, she joined them during their journey to the different cities. Through informal chatting and doing things together, she has obtained the following findings.

5. Empirical Data

When comparing with mass tourists, students have less spending capacity. Not only can they not purchase luxurious products, they are highly sensitive to the price of conventional tourist products. Secondly, as intellectuals they usually express high interest to the history, culture, architecture, art collection, reputation of the destinations. However, they are not interested in purely pastime such as gambling or dancing. Thirdly, because of their short free time, they prefer to engage in sightseeing activities instead of idleness. It means that they will not stay for a long time in one destination but travel as far and as often as possible. Fourthly, for the sake of safety and social exchange, they usually do not travel alone but form a small travel group with classmates or friends. The last but the most important specificity is that they are backpackers and do not attend local travel agency's travel tours but travel by themselves.

As backpackers, they have to make arrangements for themselves. They decide the destinations and food, transportation, hotel, etc. by themselves. Therefore, the convenience in their travel experience will directly influence their perception of a destination in some degree.

5.1 Convenience

All of them express high admiration for the Belgian railway system between cities. Purchasing the train ticket is a fairly easy undertaking.

Moreover the price is affordable, especially for the discounted tickets for youngsters below the age of 26. Travelling by train is experienced as very comfortable. The seats and the environment of the train are clean and tidy. However, there is the inconvenience of trains not running according to schedule. They experience this as a general and not a typically Belgian phenomenon. As Flemish cities are small especially in comparison to their Chinese counterparts, most students visit the different sites on foot. Although walking on cobblestones is not pleasant neither comfortable they do not mind since these cobblestones match well with the medieval architecture and the atmosphere of Flemish cities.

5.2   Travel information

The main sources of travel information include in declining order mouth-to-mouth introduction from friends, internet and tourism offices. The foremost source is through recommendation of Chinese friends, who have visited the city before. Internet is also an important source, especially for practical matters such as transportation and main attractions of a city. They also value tourism offices very highly for providing reliable and up-to-date information. The drawback is however that it is not easy to find the tourism offices. In some cities like Brussels, Ghent and Leuven, the tourism offices are not located in the train station but in the city centre. When they finally find them, they have already passed or visited most attractions of the city. To illustrate in Brussels there are two tourism offices. One office is located in the Grand Place, which is the centre area of the city. Another one is in the South railway station of Brussels. Most Chinese students arrive at the Central railway station or the North railway station in Brussels.

5.3   Language barrier

Language barrier remains somewhat a stumble block for Chinese student travellers. Chinese student travellers do not speak Dutch or French, the two official languages in Belgium. In Flanders, most people speak English but often with some accent. The serious language barrier is encountered in Brussels, where most people on the streets tend to respond in French.

Employees in tourism offices and attractions however generally are fluent in English. Meanwhile, announcements in public spaces such as train stations represent a stress factor for student travellers. As these announcements are made in Dutch or in French, they worry about missing a train or a train stop. The same applies to contacts with locals as in the case of buying souvenirs. The communication with shopkeepers is reduced to a minimalist level.

5.4 Interpretation system and guidebooks

Generally, the interpretation system consist of the intervention of the travel guides in conjunction with different kinds of material interpretation such as introduction publications, city map, interpretation board, video and recording guide. According to current conditions of the five cities, each city has its own guidebooks and tourist maps. They are readily available in local tourism offices or railway stations. Some even have a Chinese version guidebook. Historical landmarks and cultural attractions such as castles, towers, churches, museums, residences of celebrity usually are presented in separate introduction leaflets or recorded guide in Dutch, French, English and German for tourists. In addition, an interpretation board which has short introduction is usually set in main rooms or important positions. Some even provide movie guides, which introduce related important historical events. All four students valued highly these guidebooks and city maps. Especially the recorded guide is warmly welcomed. Yet the drawback is the length of the explanation. To illustrate at the Steen castle in Ghent, the movie guide of the castle lasts for 100 minutes, while their whole stay time in this castle is at most 70 minutes. Therefore, they prefer to take home the introduction materials for reading in their spare time rather than listening to the entire recording guide in the building. Meanwhile, besides the length the student travellers do not always understand the recording because of specific difficult words and sometimes they lack a general historical background of Europe. The Chinese version guidebook was of course very well received. However, it contained many language mistakes and compared to the English version, it was shorter. Thus in the end they prefer to read the English version rather than the Chinese booklet.

5.5 Four main areas of interest

Based on the empirical data, four main areas are identified as points of interest in order to assess the general perception of the five cities: museums, ancient buildings, natural scene and modern buildings and other destinations.

City	Museum	Ancient Building	Natural Scene	Modern Building and Other Destinations
Brussels	Royal Military Museum, Auto World, Museums of the Far East.	City Hall and the Grand Place, The Royal Palace The Cinquantenaire Chinatown of Brussels	Park of Brussels	The Atomium European Union
Antwerp	Diamond Museum Province of Antwerp National Maritime Museum Steen	City Hall and the Grand Place The Residence of Rubens Cathedral of our Lady and Tower China town of Antwerp	Antwerp Port and the River	The Meir Business street
Gent	Museum of Dr. Guislain	The Castle of the Counts St Bavo's Cathedral St Nicholas's church	The River Scene of the City	
Bruges	Chocolate Museum	The Historical City Centre (city hall, Grand Place and Churches)	The River Scene of the City	
Leuven		Great Beguinage. City Hall and Grand Place Churches of Leuven The Central Library of K.U.Leuven		

Fig. 3: Four main areas of interest in different cities.

5.6 Buying souvenirs

Conventionally local specialties associated with Belgium are beer, chocolate and laces. They also serve as the representative souvenirs of Belgium. In the Chinese student tourists' opinion, they think beer to be less refined and sophisticated compared to red wine. Meanwhile, they do drink the local beer of Antwerp or Brussels during their visit. However, they do not buy local beer as souvenir. Chocolate is one of the favourite snacks of most Chinese students. They are especially awed by the artisanship of chocolates, with chocolates in all forms and shape: animals, fruits, vegetables, small houses and flowers. However, they buy only a small amount because of the expensive price. Moreover, they do not seem to taste the difference between the different types of chocolates.

Undoubtedly, lace is refined, beautiful, and thus very attractive for Chinese girls. This does not necessarily mean that they purchase it because of its lack of practical use and the expensive price.

The question remains: what do they buy? According to the author's observation, most buy local post cards because they are cheap, easy to carry and full of images, which they can show to others at home. Books about local history and culture are another favourite purchase. Some buy chocolates.

5.7 Reception by locals

The level of local people's friendliness has a direct influence on the visitor's perception of the city and the visitors' choice of holiday destination, while prompting repeat visits (Gee et al., 1989). According to the author's observation, all four students do not actively interact with local people because of language barrier. Therefore, the contact with local people is limited to asking local people the way or when buying souvenirs. Overall most local people were highly friendly to the four students. Although they cannot communicate deeply because of the language barrier, the locals were keen to assist them if necessary. At the same time, some local tourism officers adopted a very professional attitude, politely smiling and patiently answering the queries of the tourists. The researcher asked the four travellers to make a list of the five cities in order of preference, while also identifying the arguments for their specific preference.

City	rank	Choice	Reason
Antwerp	No.1	4 person	Modern business atmosphere matches perfect with flourish history and culture heritage and it is very like some Chinese cities
Bruges	No.2	3 person	Beautiful natural scene and historical atmosphere
	No.3	1 person	
Leuven	No.2	1 person	Quiet, sophisticated and clean university city
	No.3	3 person	
Brussels	No.4	3 person	The capital of Belgium and European Union
	No.5	1 person	
Ghent	No.5	4 person	A big and quiet historical city, resembling Bruges

Fig.4: Impressions of different cities.

6. Some Reflections on the Empirical Findings

It is clear that the motivations of Chinese travellers, whether they are international students or mass tourists, differ greatly from their Western counterparts (Arlt 2006; Wagner 2007). They are not the usual Western vacation makers, in search of sun and sea, cultural authenticity or the marvels of nature. In fact travelling for the emergent class of Chinese tourists has more commonality with an expedition than a promise of relaxation and having fun. The difference between mass tourists and student travellers lies in the organized versus independent form of travel. Moreover, international students have more knowledge about local European cultures than mass tourists. Yet the knowledge of the former also has limits, as becomes clear from the empirical data. Mass tourists overall have more money to spend on shopping for brand items than students.

Nonetheless, there are many more similarities. First of all the prestige and brand orientation can also be found among the student population. Although the Flemish Tourism Office does not promote Brussels, they nonetheless want to visit because of its prestigious reputation as the capital of Belgium and the European Union. Brand orientation seems to apply to students too. When comparing wine to beer, they would place wine higher and more sophisticated than beer. In the postmodern, post-industrial societies, the strict division between the superior wine and the more plebeian beer seem not to make any sense as regarding beer there is also the niche market of gourmet beer. In addition, the postmodern cultural class, the bourgeois bohemians seem to have developed a taste for simple, locally made (brewed) products (Zukin 2006). The comparative tendency with China also applies to Chinese student tourists. They have a specific preference for the streetscape of Meir in Antwerp as it reminds them of major cities in China. According to lifestyle magazines in Belgium, this street is by no means the most trendy or upbeat street. On the contrary, it is categorized as a highly commercial street filled with mass produced goods in chain stores. In terms of immersion versus gaze, they do not differ radically from the mass tourists. They show very little patience with the historical accounts provided by museums. Said differently they do not gain an in-depth knowledge of local material and immaterial cultural heritage. As for mass tourists, their visit consists of a quick glance rather than in-depth immersion.

They also have a liking for superlatives. They make a list of top destinations and landmarks. Once a landmark is labelled the best, there is no need to see another similar landmark. After seeing the museum of Diamonds in Antwerp, which they claim to be the best museum, they do not feel the need to visit other museum of diamonds in other cities. Some call this process 'image defilation'[62].

In terms of signage, they appreciate the effort of Chinese language information brochures. However, at the same time they show no mercy for the language mistakes in the Chinese text.

[62] Yang Zhenzi, Chen Jin, *Tourism Tribune*: A Theoretical and Positive Research on the Core Part of Image Machination of Tourist Destination:"Image Defilation" and "Image Superposition", 2003(3).

References

Appadurai, Arjun (ed) (1986) *The Social Life of Things: Commodities in Cultural Perspective.* Cambridge: Cambridge University Press.

Arlt, Wolfgang G. (2006) *China' Outbound Tourism.* Oxford: Routledge.

Arlt, Wolfgang G. & Freyer, W. (2008) *Deutschland als Reiseziel Chinesischer Touristen Chancen für den deutschen Reisemarkt.* Oldenbourg Wissenschaftsverlag GmbH.

CNTA (ed.) (2006) *the Yearbook of China Tourism Statistics.* Beijing: China Tourism Press.

CNTA (ed.) (2008) *the Yearbook of China Tourism Statistics.* Beijing: China Tourism Press.

Bourdieu, Pierre (1984) *Distinction. A Social Critique of the Judgement of Taste.* London: Routledge.

Featherstone, Mike (1991) *Consumer Culture and Postmodernism.* London: Sage.

Ferguson, Harvie (1990) *The Science of Pleasure: Cosmos and Psyche in the Bourgeois World View.* London: Routledge.

Freedman, Jonathan L. (1981) *Social Psychology.* Englewood Cliffs (N.J.): Prentice-Hall.

Freyer, Tony A. (2006) *Antitrust and Global Capitalism, 1930-2004.* New York: Cambridge University Press.

Gartner, William C. & Hunt, John D. (1987) an Analysis of State Image Change over a Twelve-Year Period (1971-1983).*Journal of Travel Research*, 20(3): 35-49.

Gudykunst, William B. & Kim, Young Yun (1997) *Communicating with strangers: an approach to intercultural communication.* Boston (Mass.): McGraw-Hill.

Hannerz, Ulf (2002) *Cultural Complexity: Studies in the Social Organization of Meaning.* New York: Columbia University Press.

Krech, David & Crutchfield, Richard S. (1948) *Theory and problems of social psychology.* New York: MacGraw-Hill.

Latham, Kevin & Thompson, Stuart & Klein, Jakob (2006) *Consuming China: Approaches to Cultural Change in Contemporary China.* Abingdon: Routledge.

Link, Perry, Madsen, Richard P. & Pickowicz, Paul.G (2002) (eds) *Popular China: Unofficial Culture in a Globalising Society.* Lanham: Rowman & Littlefield.

Liu, Kang (2004) *Globalization and Cultural Trends in China.* Honolulu: University of Hawaii.

Nesbitt, Richard E. (2004) *The Geography of Thought. How Asians and Westerners think differently and why.* Illinois: Free Press.

Pearce, Philip L. (1980) Favorability-satisfaction model of tourists' evaluation. *Journal of Travel Research.* 14(1): 13-17.

Pearce, Philip L. (1982) The Social Psychology of Tourist Behavior, *International Series in Experimental Social Psychology.* Vol. 3. Oxford: Pergamon Press.

Perry, John (1978) *A Dialogue on Personal Identity and Immortality.* Indianapolis: Hackett Publishing Company.

Phelps, Edmund S. (1986) *Economic Equilibrium and Other Economic Concepts: a New Palgrave Quartet.* Florence: European university institute. Department of economics.

Pizam, Abraham & Calantone, Roger (1991) Beyond psychographics- values as determinants of tourist behavior. *International Journal of Hospitality Management* 6(3): 177-181.

Reisinger, Yvette & Turner, Lindsay (1990) Structural equation modeling with LISREL: Application in Tourism. *Tourism Management.* 24(5):575-585.

Roberstson, Thomas S. (1970) *Consumer Behavior.* Glenview : Scott, Foresman.

Nemetz-Robinson, Gail L. (1988) *Crosscultural understanding.* New York: Prentice Hall.

Rokeach, Milton. *The open and closed mind: investigations into the nature of belief systems and personality systems.* New York : Basic Books.

Samover, Larry A., Porter, Richard E. & McDaniel, Edwin R. (1991) *Communication between Cultures.* Belmont, CA: Wadsworth Publishing.

Schiffman, Leon G. & Kanuk, Leslie L. (1987) *Consumer Behavior.* Englewood Cliffs (N.J.): Prentice Hall international.

Urry, John (1990) *The Tourists Gaze: Leisure and Travel in Contemporary Societies.* London, Sage:3.

Wagner, Wieland *Chinese tourists do Europe –in 14 days.* 8.17.2007
http://www.spiegel.de/international/europe/0,1518,500550,00.html.

Wu, Dingbo & Murphy, Patrick (1994) *Handbook of Chinese Popular Culture.* Westport, Connecticut, London: Green Wood Press.

Xinhua News Agency (2009)
http://news.xinhuanet.com/world/200902/17/content/_10830173.htm.

Yu, Xin & Weiler, Betty (2001) Mainland Chinese Pleasure Travellers to Australia: A Leisure Behavior Analysis. *Tourism, Culture & Communication*, 3, 81–93.

Yum, June. O. (1988) *the Impact of Confucianism on Interpersonal Relationships and Communication Patterns in East Asia*. Communication Monographs, 55, 374-388.

Zukin, Sharon (2008) Consuming authenticity. *Cultural Studies*, 22 (5), 724-748.

Schleswig-Holstein (Germany) as a destination for Chinese Outbound travellers

Wolfgang Georg Arlt

1. Introduction

Schleswig-Holstein is the northernmost state of Germany. Flanked on the west by the North Sea and on the east by the Baltic Sea, Schleswig-Holstein occupies the southern part of the Jutland peninsula and extends from the Elbe River and Hamburg northward to the Danish border. With a population of less than three million people, 5.7 million tourist arrivals show the importance of tourism as one of the major industries in the state "between the seas"(Statistik Nord 2009).

China and Germany, the two most important export economies in the world, have intensive economic relations with exports from Germany to China reaching 50 billion US$ (2008) and exports from China to Germany even 87 Billion US$ (2008). Tourism relations are also growing with about half a million travellers per year going each way (DZT 2009). Schleswig-Holstein plays an active role in Chinese-German economic relationships and has partnered with the province of Zhejiang since 1986. In 1999 a "Schleswig-Holstein Business Center" opened its doors in Hangzhou and a number of companies as well as universities have developed closed trade, production and research links. Tourism, especially from China to Schleswig-Holstein, has however not followed the general pattern of growth with the number of Chinese visitors to the state remaining below 2,500 in 2008. Not even 1% of the Chinese visitors to Germany find their way across the Elbe River.

To attract more Chinese travellers, it is obviously necessary to adapt the offered tourism products and the marketing channels and messages to their specific needs and expectations.

These chapters briefly looks at the framework and general conditions of Chinese tourism to Germany before analysing the existing major attractions of Schleswig-Holstein and their fit with the demand structure of Chinese leisure tourists. Using the results of a study conducted in 2008 by Wolfgang Georg Arlt and Leonie Friedlein (Arlt, Friedlein 2008)

117

for the Schleswig-Holstein Tourism Agency TASH, the Chamber of Commerce Kiel and the Marketing Cooperation Cities in Schleswig-Holstein MAKS it aims to identify the most promising ways of increasing the attractiveness of the region for Chinese leisure tourists.

2.   Development of China's Outbound Tourism

In Imperial China, travelling was considered as an important part of the personal education as well as a common leisure activity for the members of the elite of the society. Travelling outside the country, however, remained the rare exception, neither adventurers nor traders or missionaries ventured beyond the border.

After the foundation of the People's Republic of China in 1949, tourism was considered as a wasteful, bourgeois and potentially dangerous activity and outbound travels were restricted to a handful of diplomats and scientists.

Only after the implementation of the policy of "Reform and Opening" in 1978, tourism was considered an instrument to support the modernisation of the country. Inbound tourism was supported as an easy way to earn hard currencies especially from tourists from Western countries and Japan, and also as a possibility to re-establish links with the Overseas Chinese communities abroad. Domestic tourisms developed spontaneously and against the will of the central government. Only in the 1990s tourism was recognized as a "pillar industry" which could support the economic development as well as the national identity and unity of China.

In preparation of the return of Hong Kong the first official outbound tourism policy was published in 1983. Citizens of the border province Guangdong could visit relatives in the then British colony. Based on this policy, visits to Macao, Thailand, Singapore, Malaysia and the Philippines, often without a real family visit background, became possible in the following decade. Another way to leave China temporarily existed in the form of visits to the bordering regions of Russia, Mongolia, Vietnam, Burma and Laos which developed during the same period.

For long-distance travel the growing integration of China into the global economy provided opportunities for delegations to visit business partners, fairs or training programs which more often than not included major parts of leisure tourism activities. Altogether, these different forms of outbound travel boosted the number of border crossings to 7.6 million by the year 1996 (Arlt 2006).

Official leisure tourism was recognized by the government in 1997 and the so-called Approved Destination System installed, which resulted in agreements with destinations for the issuing of tourists group visa for Chinese citizens. After the turn of the century the number of such "open" destinations grows ever faster until with the USA and Canada the latest major destinations, were included. The procedures to attain a passport, the right to exchange Chinese RMB into other currencies, and the requirements for tour operators to offer outbound trips were simplified more and more and a heated and sometimes chaotic period of growth followed, bringing the number of border crossings to 10 million in the year 2000, only to double to 20 million in 2003 and again to 40 million in 2007. In 2009 almost 48 million trips were recorded (Xinhua 2010), albeit with 2/3 of them terminating already in Hong Kong or Macao.

3. Development of China's Outbound Tourism to Germany

Germany evolved early on as an important business partner for China and therefore also as a major "delegation tourism" destination in the 1980s and 1990s. The number of visits from China increased in absolute figures, but the relative share of Germany as part of the total Chinese outbound tourism decreased in the last decade.

With the exception of Malta, Germany was the first European country which signed an ADS agreement with China. The expected boom in 2003 however was prevented by the SARS crisis, leaving the 2002 number of arrivals almost unchanged at around 270,000. This figure rose to almost 420,000 in 2005 and more than 460,000 in 2007. In the following year the arrival numbers went back to the 2005 level due to the global economic crisis, but the number of overnight stays remained almost stable with 950,000 in 2007 and 943.000 in 2008. These figures also indicate that the average length of stay in Germany is not much longer than two nights, because for most, especially leisure tourists, Germany is just one stop on a multi-destination trip to Europe.

119

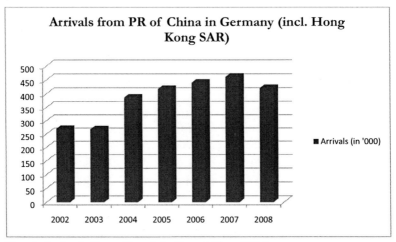

Arrivals from PR of China in Germany (incl. Hong Kong SAR)

■ Arrivals (in '000)

Fig. 1: Arrivals from People's Republic of China
in Germany 2002-2008 (including Hong Kong SAR)[63]

The destinations of Chinese visitors are mostly located in the Southern and Western part of Germany. The states Bayern, Hesse, Nordrhein-Westfalia, Baden-Wuerttemberg, Rheinland-Palatine and Berlin are responsible for almost 90% of all Chinese overnight stays in Germany. Within the states the big cities are the most important places of visit. The "Magic Cities" of Berlin, Cologne, Dresden, Düsseldorf, Frankfurt, Hamburg, Hannover, Leipzig, Munich and Stuttgart alone can welcome almost half of all Chinese visitors. The northern part of Germany, with the notable exception of Hamburg, are profiting less from the increase of Chinese visitors to Germany.

---

[63] DZT 2009.

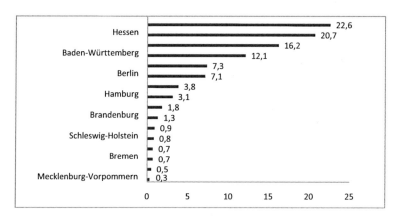

Fig. 2: Overnight stays of Chinese visitors (including Hong Kong SAR) in German states 2007 (in %)[64]

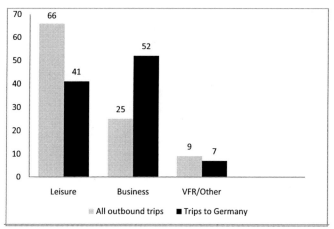

Fig. 3: Main motivation of Chinese outbound travellers for travel (2007)[65]

Germany is still the most important destination for Chinese travellers in Europe, excepting Russia, where most Chinese visitors actually arrive in

---

[64] DZT 2009.
[65] DZT 2009.

the Asian part of Russia. More than half of the visitors are business travellers, whereas "Visiting Friends and Relatives" motivates only 7% for a trip to Germany. This structure is very different if compared to the overall figures for Chinese outbound travellers, which include the visitors to Hong Kong and Macao SARs.

The age structure of visitors is accordingly also different with less old and more middle-aged persons travelling to Germany compared to the overall figures. As a visit to Germany is still only affordable for the top tier of the Chinese society, which includes a number of approximately 60 to 80 million people, almost all Chinese visitors to Germany have a comparatively high level of income and education.

Most Chinese visitors have a very distinct image of Germany, which is normally re-enforced during their trip by the itinerary and the explanations of the Chinese tour guides. Element of the image include Germany as an industrial country of capable engineers producing machines and cars as well as Germany as the home of beer, medieval city centres, fairy tales and famous composers of classical music. Safety and good organizations are also often mentioned as positive elements of the image. Germany as the birthplace of Karl Marx on the other hand is loosing its appeal especially for younger visitors. Most Chinese visitors are surprised by the beauty and diversity of the nature that can be found and may opt for a boat trip on the River Rhine. Coastal areas with a more Northern European feeling to them as can be found in Schleswig-Holstein, are however not a part of the Germany image of most Chinese visitors. Another aspect of Germany is certainly the possibility to shop for "traditional" regional items and for famous branded goods. 13% of all Tax Free Shopping turnovers in Germany (2008) are created by the Chinese fondness of shopping (Arlt, Freyer 2008).

4. Development of China's Outbound Tourism to Schleswig-Holstein

Tourism in Schleswig-Holstein is mainly dominated by domestic leisure tourists. 88.6% (2008) of all arrivals are from German visitors. Among the 11.4% inbound tourists, Europe again strongly dominates with 10.7% of all arrivals. Just 0.7% is of non-European nationalities, made up mostly of American (0.3%) and Asian (0.2%) passport holders. This situation has been more or less stable in the last years.

The number of Chinese visitors to Schleswig-Holstein is small, but at least it has been growing in recent years. The average length of stay is also longer compared with the German average with rather three than two nights. From 2004 to 2008, the number of arrivals almost doubled from almost 1,300 to more than 2,400. Until now the highest number of overnight stays was recorded for 2007 with close to 8,000 nights. In 2008, 9% of all non-European visitors and 23% of all Asian visitors to Schleswig-Holstein were Chinese or Hong Kong passport holders (Nord Statistik 2009).

Year	Arrivals	Over-night stays	Average length of stay
2003	1084	3445	3.2
2004	1282	3855	3.0
2005	1512	4926	3.3
2006	1806	5334	3.0
2007	2033	7987	4.0
2008	2420	5739	2.4

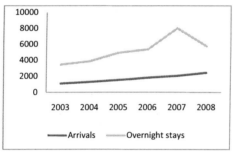

Fig. 4: Arrivals, overnight stays and average length of stay Chinese visitors (including Hong Kong SAR) in Schleswig-Holstein 2004-2008[66]

However, a closer look at the regional structure of these visits reveals that almost half of these stays are probably rather due to the fact that tour operators for financial reasons use hotels just across the border from the city state of Hamburg than to a genuine interest of the visitors in Schleswig-Holstein.

---

[66] Nord Statistik 2009.

Not only the spatial distribution of Chinese visitors is very different from the German tourists in Schleswig-Holstein, also the seasonality is much less pronounced on the Chinese side. Obviously, unlike the majority of the domestic tourists, Chinese visitors to Schleswig-Holstein are not interested in summer beach life on the two coasts of the state.

5. Analysis of possible attractions for Chinese visitors to Schleswig-Holstein

As a precondition for a more successful targeting of the Chinese outbound market, destinations, attractions and activities were selected in a study and analysed according to their attractiveness for Chinese visitors and the possibilities of product adaptation for their specific demand. There is obviously a growing group of sophisticated, well-travelled Chinese tourists with deeper knowledge about and interest in Europe and European culture. The study concentrated nevertheless more on the majority of visitors who visit Germany as a part of a trip to several European countries and cannot be considered as holiday-makers.

Following earlier studies by the author (Arlt 2006, Arlt, Freyer 2008) as well as by other researchers, experts interviews and a focus group of Chinese students in Schleswig-Holstein, a list of six criteria was selected:

- Level of popularity and fame
- Uniqueness
- Entertainment value
- Typicality for the region
- Connection to China
- Accessibility

Each criterion was weighed according to the importance for Chinese visitors to Schleswig-Holstein giving a weight of "5" for a), b) and d), "4" for c) and f) and "3" for e).

All destinations and activities were analysed using the below criteria, with points given for every occurrence of the aspects listed. If a single aspect occurred in a specially pronounced way, an extra point could be assigned. The value achieved for each criterion was then multiplied with the importance for Chinese visitors. An overachievement did not result in extra points. The maximum number of possible points was 130. The results were visualized in a graph.

For each criterion five possible aspects were selected:

Level of popularity and fame	English language website Chinese language website Mentioned as highlight on National Tourism Board website Host of international events UNESCO World Heritage Site
Uniqueness	USP (unique selling proposition) Unique in natural, historical or cultural sense Unique in Germany Unique in Europe Unique photo opportunity
Entertainment value	Story connected to sight Presentations Hands-on activities Games, Quiz etc. Guided tour in typical or historical costumes
Typicality for the region	Shipping/Sailing Historical connection to Hanse / Vikings etc. Typical for Schleswig-Holstein or Northern Germany Typical product Supraregional association
Connection to China	Historical connection Place of visit by famous Chinese Economic, cultural or other cooperation City partnership Local Overseas Chinese community
Accessibility	Rail connection Highway connection Highway connection to important transit routes) Harbour for ferries / cruise ships Airport

Fig. 5: Five aspects of 6 interest criteria

Using information of the German National Tourism Board, experts' interviews and a focus group of Chinese students in Schleswig-Holstein, a list of 15 possible sights and activities was selected for the analysis. These were:

Lübeck	Eutin Castle
Kiel	Tidal flat landscape hiking
Rendsburg	Karl-May festival
Oldenburg in Holstein	Touristic Routes
Schleswig	Multimar Wattforum
Flensburg	Kappeln
Glücksburg Castle	Famous persons
Plön Castle	

Fig.6: 15 possible sights

As examples of the achieved results, the results for the four top destinations of the study are briefly presented. Only these four of the surveyed destinations and activities reached 65 points out of the possible maximum of 130 points, clearly showing that the almost total concentration on customers from Germany and neighbouring countries in the tourism industry as well as sometimes a lack of accessibility prevents the full utilization of the touristic potential of many possible tourism products for non-Western visitors in Schleswig-Holstein.

5.1 Lübeck

The Hanseatic City of Lübeck came up top in the study as the most attractive destination for Chinese visitors. The main reason is the historical city centre, which has been designated as an UNESCO World Heritage Site since 1987. This distinction and the picturesque character of the historic buildings and the museum harbour is fitting very well with the expectations of the visitors. The sweet almost paste Marzipan provides a nice typical local souvenir. The German famous persons connected to Lübeck are unknown and therefore of less interest to the majority of Chinese visitors.

Lübeck is actively promoted itself in China as a member of the regional "China Tourism Pool" and offers a Chinese language website. Only the criterion "Entertainment Value" shows clearly room for improvement and should be taken care of.

	Fame	Uniqueness	Entertainment	Typicality	China connection	Accessibility	Total
Lübeck	25	20	4	25	6	20	100

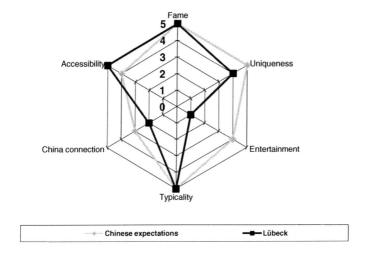

Fig. 7: Lübeck as a travel destination

127

5.2 Kiel

The capital of Schleswig-Holstein, Kiel, achieved a level of publicity because of its support of Qingdao as the venue for the Olympic sailing competitions. This connection fits well with the other mostly maritime attractions of Kiel. As the main harbour for cruise ships, the city can also offer the opportunity for short cruises including shopping opportunities on board.

Beer is an important part of the German image and the "beer diploma" offered by the Kiel Brewery would be attractive for Chinese visitors, if it can be achieved in a short time and without the necessity to understand the German language. Kiel is another example of only partly utilized potential given its political importance, good accessibility and beautiful location.

	Fame	Unique-ness	Entertain-ment	Typicality	China connection	Accessi-bility	Total
Kiel	15	15	8	15	9	16	78

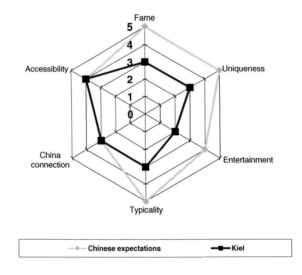

Fig. 8: Kiel as a travel destination

128

5.3 Rendsburg

Rendsburg is located at the centre of the Kiel canal, which connects the Baltic Sea and the Atlantic Ocean. The main attraction here is an unique technical museum piece still working: a suspension ferry over the canal which is suspended from the railway bridge. Bridge and ferry were constructed almost 100 years ago, the bridge is one of the biggest in Europe and the cabin transporting passengers free of charge over the canal is hanging on steel cables just four meters over the water.

Other attractions of Rendsburg include a medieval city centre and the Kiel Canal itself, the most heavily used artificial seaway in the world. Clear deficits are recognisable in the lack of marketing activities towards international visitors. A useful job for a historian would be the search for Chinese celebrities who visited the Kiel Canal or Rendsburg in earlier times.

	Fame	Uniqueness	Entertainment	Typicality	China connection	Accessibility	Total
Rendsburg	10	20	12	15	0	12	69

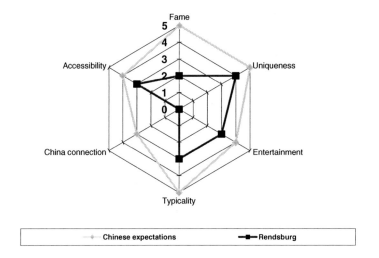

Fig. 9: Rendsburg as a travel destination

129

5.4 Famous personalities – Friedrichsruh

Following in the footsteps of famous persons and celebrities is a major motivators for Chinese tourists. Schleswig-Holstein is proud about a number of great sons of the region who are however not necessarily known to Chinese visitors. The museums, birthplaces and memorials for authors like Theodor Storm or Thomas Mann or politicians like Willy Brandt hold little attraction except for experts, even though Mann and Brandt received Nobel prices for literature and peace respectively.

An exception could be Alfred Nobel himself. His invention of dynamite took place in Krümmel on the Schleswig-Holstein bank of the River Elbe, which was the location of Nobel's biggest factory for explosives. Unfortunately the site was demolished after 1945 and later used for the construction of a nuclear power plant. More attractive is a visit to Friedrichsruh Castle, home of Otto von Bismarck, who in 1896 hosted the famous reformer and politician of the Qing Dynasty Li Hongzhang here for a well-documented visit. The analysis was done accordingly for Friedrichsruh.

	Fame	Unique ness	Entertain- ment	Typicality	China connection	Accessibil- ity	Total
Friedrichsruh	5	15	8	10	9	20	69

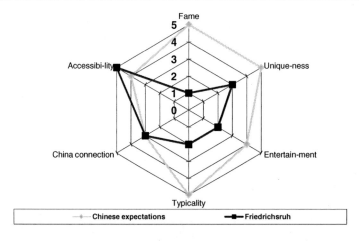

Fig. 10: Friedsruh as a travel destination

6. Conclusion

This chapter tried to analyse, based on an overview about the development of Chinese outbound tourism especially to Germany and to Schleswig-Holstein in particular, the existing tourism offers in Schleswig-Holstein from the point of view of Chinese leisure tourists. With the results of the analysis and the survey we can now evaluate the specific potential of the state for this source market to attract – alone or in connection with other destinations – visitors from China.

There can be no doubt that China as a tourism source market is gaining more and more importance in international tourism. In 2009 China's outbound tourism continued to grow by 4% to 48 million border crossings, while most other major tourism source markets recorded negative growth rates. About 5% of international travellers are originating from Mainland China and another 1% from Hong Kong SAR and Taiwan. For Germany China and Japan are the most important Asian source markets in tourism (UNWTO 2009).

The data also show that Chinese visitors could help to fill up spatial and temporal demand gaps, as they are not very interested in summer beach holidays like the majority of holiday visitors to the state. This offers opportunities for development for destinations not located on the coasts and for off-season periods. The majority of Chinese visitors are travelling in organized groups, making it easier to foresee and organize services for them. Furthermore Chinese visitors tend to spend more per day if compared to German tourists or to other international visitors.

At the moment Schleswig-Holstein is not utilizing the possibilities of non-Europeans, especially Chinese, inbound tourism as the total percentage of transcontinental arrivals staying below 1% of all arrivals unmistakably proves.

The image problem of Schleswig-Holstein is an image problem of Northern Germany: The stereotypes about Germany are build on Bavaria and the River Rhine area, the more "Scandinavian" feeling of the coastal areas are not connected to Germany in the same way. This problem is aggravated by the demand of Chinese visitors for a fast sequence of famous sights, a lot of photo opportunities and a respectful treatment of Chinese culture.

Only for 15 surveyed, tourism offers achieved more than 50% of the possible maximum number of points: Lübeck, Kiel, Rendsburg and Friedrichsruh. For everybody offers popularity, entertainment value and connections to China showing the biggest gaps between the expectations of Chinese visitors and the touristic offers and the marketing around them.

Transcontinental marketing efforts are mainly based on the work of the German National Tourism Board and especially the German Coast-line marketing association as well as the Hamburg-based China Tourism Pool. These activities have shown already some positive results, which are however for Schleswig-Holstein mainly concentrated on the old Hanseatic city of Lübeck.

To increase the entertainment value a greater eventisation, the creation of experiences which can be captured by photo and video, and a connection of attractions with stories and images which are comprehensible for Chinese visitors, seems necessary. To establish a connection to China through historical or current economic, academic or cultural aspects should be possible for most destinations. Friedrichsruh is a good example for an event like the visit of Li Hongzhang, which is not very interesting for other visitors, but might act as a major motivation for Chinese tourists to visit this place.

For most Chinese travellers Schleswig-Holstein will remain one stop on a bigger trip to Germany or even parts of Europe. Within such round trips Schleswig-Holstein is however able to use the proximity of Hamburg as a major destination for Chinese visitors as well as the growing number of repeat travellers from China who visit Scandinavia or the Baltic Sea region. For these visitors Schleswig-Holstein can offer points of contact in a geographical sense as well as in a thematic sense as part of themed tours about the Hanse trading association, the Viking Empire and so on.

The question about the potential of the existing tourism offers in Schleswig-Holstein from the point of view of Chinese leisure tourists can accordingly be answered with several insights:

- Using Lübeck und Kiel as regional "anchors", the potential of Schleswig-Holsteins to attract Chinese visitors, especially those who visit Europe not for the first time, is sufficient. However, the existing destinations and offers can not be marketed by themselves but only in a close spatial and thematic interlocking.

- This should include not only attractions within Schleswig-Holstein but also destinations in other parts of Northern Germany and Northern Europe.

- Attracting Chinese visitors can be seen as a part of the necessary internationalization of the tourism offers of Schleswig-Holstein including the proliferation of English language websites and brochures and a larger number of English speaking staff.

- To be successful, product adaptation according to the specific expectations and interests of the Chinese visitors is as necessary as a concentration of resources of several destinations for a target-group specific marketing.

- Existing economic and academic relations between Schleswig-Holstein and China can be used to support tourism marketing, for example in the field of wind power and with student exchanges, as well as unconventional marketing efforts like offering a summer training camp for young Chinese team handball player, an olympic sport discipline for which Schleswig-Holstein is famous.

- Investment of resources into the Chinese market is making sense not only because of the size and potential further growth of the source market but also because Chinese visitors can be used to ease seasonal and spatial imbalances in the demand of the majority domestic visitors.

- It is not necessary to try to orient all tourism providers towards the target group of Chinese visitors. As most of them are travelling in organized groups, they, or more precisely the inbound tour operators organizing the tour, can be guided towards attractions which have an interest in this target group.

- Accordingly the most promising step towards a rectification of the leeway of Schleswig-Holstein in this market seems to be the installation of a pool of private and public stakeholders interested in attracting Chinese customers to their offers.

References

Arlt, Wolfgang G. (2006): *China's Outbound Tourism*. London/New York.

Arlt, Wolfgang G./Freyer, Walter (2008) (Hg.): *Deutschland als Reiseziel chinesischer Touristen*. München.

Arlt, Wolfgang G./Friedlein, L. (2008): *Schleswig-Holstein als Reiseziel für Gäste aus der Volksrepublik China*. Heide.

DZT Deutsche Zentrale für Tourismus e.V. (2009) (Hg.): *Incoming-Tourismus Deutschland. Edition 2009*. Frankfurt/Main.

Statistik-Nord (2009): 02.01.2010. http://www.Statistik-Nord.de.

UNWTO (2009): *UNWTO Tourism Highlights 2009 Edition*. 02.02.2010. http://www.unwto.org/facts/eng/pdf/highlights/UNWTO_Highlights09_en_LR.pdf.

Xinhua (2010): *China's tourism revenue hits $185 bln in 2009*. 07.01.2010. http://www.xinhuanet.com.

How to Successfully and Cost Effectively Market Foreign Destinations in China

Adam Wu

Amid the fast growing importance and the shear size of the Chinese outbound travel market many destinations on the national, regional and even some local level have been trying to reach the lucrative Chinese outbound market. Different destinations have tried out different ways of marketing their destinations and have had different experiences and often with different outcomes that lead them to draw different conclusions some can be very discouraging drown often from the experience of much money spent without achieving the objective. This article tries to shed some light on how to successfully and cost effectively promote foreign destination in China.

1. Dilemma faced by foreign tourism promotion authorities in marketing foreign destinations in the vast Chinese market

With a surge of outbound visitors from mere 9 million in 1999 to 46 million in less than 10 years which represents more than 500% increase or doubles every three years and treble every five year as confirmed by the graph below, few destination promotion authorities would not be tempted trying to reach this fastest growing market which still has vast potential.

135

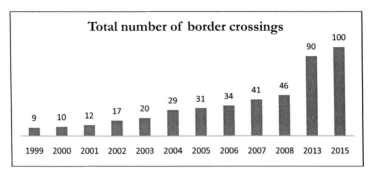

Fig.1: Total number of border crossings of Chinese citizens 1999- 2015 (2013 and 2015: estimates)

1.1 The lucrative and fast growing Chinese outbound market

Indeed, the 46 million border crossings in 2008 represented only about 3.5% of the total population of over 1.3 billion. With various sources claiming that China already has as many as 100 million people having the spending power of middle class[67] rising to 600 million by 2015, it is becoming too obvious for foreign destinations to be eager to attract those would be spenders. However, experience demonstrates that marketing foreign destinations especially with very different tourism products and services can face a number of difficulties with "Chinese characteristics".

1.1.1 Language Barrier

Contrary to some reports, China has about only 10 million English speakers[68], which is a smaller number if compared to Poland where 11 million speaks English fluently (representing 29% of the total population). However, only 0.77% of the Chinese population is able to use English for meaningful communication. This is far below the 100 million or so Chinese who wish to travel overseas currently. Even among the travel professionals very few senior (both in term of position and age) decision makers speak any foreign language. Although an increasing number of young (often junior) and operations staff have learned Eng-

---

[67] http://www.wikinvest.com/concept/Rise_of_China's_Middle_Class.
[68] http://en.wikipedia.org/wiki/List_of_countries_by_English
- speaking_population.

lish, most of those tend to prefer using Chinese when communicate for business purposes for fear of not speaking well or simply for understanding better in their own language. This is more like the native Spanish speakers who prefer using their native language, even those who can speak English well.

Of course, those who like arguing can always point to some Chinese speaking very well English. However, the compiling evidence of only 10 million English speakers in China is too small a proportion for foreign tourism promotion authorities to justify using other than Chinese language in order to communicate key messages and promote destinations in China. Not surprisingly even the United Nations World Tourism Organisation (UNWTO) has listed Chinese as one of its official languages [69]

1.1.2 Large Territory

China is as almost as big as the entire Europe combined with twice as many population. Many tourism promotion authorities have to attend major exhibitions in some key markets throughout Europe from Finland to France, from Germany to Greece in order to cover not even all European countries. Not surprisingly China alone has over 10 international travel exhibitions in different cities throughout the year such as:

- Nanjing Travel EXPO, Nanjing, 22-23.03, 2010
- Guangzhou International Travel Fair (GITF), Guangzhou, 25-27.03, 2010
- China Outbound Travel and Tourism Market (COTTM), Beijing, 27-29.04, 2010
- World Expo 2010 Shanghai, Shanghai, 01.05- 31.10, 2010
- World Travel Fair (WTF), Shanghai, 27-29.05, 2010
- Beijing International Tourism Expo (BITE), Beijing, 18-21.06, 2010
- Qingdao International Tourism Expo (QITE), Qingdao, 21-23.08, 2010
- Jinan International Travel Fair, Jinan, 04-06.09, 2010
- China Incentive Business Travel & Meetings Exhibition (CIBTM), Beijing, 07-09.09, 2010
- World Tourism Destination Fair, Tianjin, 18-20.09, 2010

---

[69] http://news.travel168.net/_En/2007_12_04_16/200712416933112.htm.

- China International Travel Mart (CITM), Shanghai, 18-21.11, 2010

Most of those exhibitions originated from promoting inbound travel to China although increasing number of travel exhibitions in China start adding element of outbound travel however, most are still often open to visiting public who are more interested in collecting souvenirs and/or brochures for selling as recycling papers rather than using them for planning overseas trips. Unfortunately, it is impossible for foreign tourism promotion authorities and travel businesses to attend all or most of the exhibitions in China due to the fact that each exhibition costs money and time.

Even those countries that invested much more money in setting up national tourist offices in China soon realised that one office in Beijing often finds difficulty to cover Shanghai and Guangzhou or other parts of China. As a result, some more determined countries notably Malaysia has tourism promotion offices in as many as four cities including Chengdu. This is just about matching China having National Tourist Office (CNTO) in London, Frankfurt, Paris, Madrid and now in Italy in order to cover key markets of Europe. Most people would agree that very few countries have the resources to maintain as many as four or more national tourist offices in China.

1.1.3 Less Developed Outbound Travel Trade
Some foreign destinations with more marketing budget tried to organise own road shows in China with the good intention of trying to reach targeted travel trade in selected cities. The experience and result seem to be mixed because the outbound travel trade in China is less developed and certainly not well organised. First of all there is little distinction between tour operators and travel agents. Most travel businesses are called Travel Service like China Travel Service or China International Travel Service and so on. Indeed, most travel services try to play both the role of a tour operator i.e. to package tours and also travel agents by selling their tour packages directly as well as through other travel services.

Furthermore, most outbound operators originated from providing inbound services or simply constitute only the outbound department of large travel services that are either subsidiaries of some major businesses like CITS Head Office, CTS Holdings or some franchised businesses covering different geographical area such as Comfort Travel Beijing, CYTS Guangdong etc.

To add further confusion there are thousands of businesses often registered not as travel services but as providing services to groups of government officials and corporate executives that need more services such as arranging invitation letters, organising events such as MICE etc that many traditional tour operators are not equipped or experienced to provide. Therefore, many of those business consulting firms operate as corporate travel organisers.

However, these corporate travel organisers are not counted for among the over 760 or so ADS operators authorised by the China National Tourism Administration (CNTA) that are meant to send leisure travellers for group travel overseas. Since most foreign tourism promotion authorities and travel businesses tend to focus on the "approved" tour operators, they are unwittingly missing out large number of potential targets who are often sending the most lucrative Chinese clients who have privileges and higher spending power (i.e. the officials and business executives).

2. Online marketing proven to be the most cost effective way of promoting foreign destinations in China

Having highlighted those difficulties with Chinese characteristics does not mean there is no better way of marketing foreign destinations in China. As a matter of fact, a number of independent surveys concluded that online marketing proven to be the most cost effective way of marketing foreign destinations in China.

Back in 2007 PATA commissioned a survey to AC Nelsen regarding the preferred sources of information of Chinese travellers and travel trade. This survey revealed that "7 out of 10 Chinese leisure travellers preferred to get informed through websites, and about 6 out of 10 using online travel discussion forums. Conducted in October 2007, the survey covered all outbound leisure and business trips taken over a 12-month period between 2006 and 2007".[70]

Since then the number of Chinese online (Netizens) grow further to have overtaken USA at the end of 2008 hence became world number one country in terms of online users. By June 2009 the number of Chi-

---

[70] PATA and AC Nielson.

nese getting online stood at 338 million which is greater than the total population of the USA[71] Rapid economic growth, and allied expansion in internet access in more areas, has fuelled the rapid rise in use of the web around China, which still have huge potential for growth for the population of over 1.3 billion.

2.1   Internet development in China

Like most other developments in China the popularity and growth of the Internet in China was also closely linked to the government policies and relevant regulations. While the internet experienced fast growth in many Western countries during the second part of 1990s when relevant authorities in China realised the real potential of the Internet and its implication in communication and distribution of information it was only on the 22nd January 1999 that the first nationwide campaign called "Government (Getting) Online Project" was jointly launched by more than 40 ministries and ministry level Administration Bureau such as CNTA led by the State Economic and Trade Commission, and then called Ministry of Information Industries which shows the level of importance that Chinese Government gives to information technology. Central government further encouraged authorities of provincial and municipal level to get online as well.

Building on the success of the "Government Online Project" second campaign called "Enterprise Online Project" was launched on the 7th July 2000 i.e. mere one and half year later to encourage and facilitate commercial companies getting on line. With another less than one and half year the Government backed "Home Online Project" was launched with direct support of the Ministry of Information Industries, Ministry of Science and Ministry of Culture as well as All China Women Federation, China Youth League Central Committee.

Knowing this early development of Internet in China one would find easier understand the surge of Internet usage in China from 2000 as demonstrated by the graph below.[72]

---

[71] China Internet Network Information Center (CNNIC):
   http://chinadigitaltimes.net/china/internet-growth.
[72] ETC new Media Trend Watch: http://www.newmediatrendwatch.com.

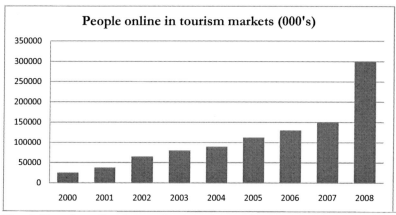

Fig. 2: People online in tourism markets (000's)

2.2   Internet in China – the China Wide Web

As a result of such Government backed campaigns China created its own nationwide computer network initially called ChinaNet so as to distinguish from the initial import of the term Internet which was to mean the World Wide Web (that is 世界互联网 in Chinese). As a result, a new phrase 中国互联网 has been used to describe the computer network in China especially those interlinked by the three nationwide campaigns that effectively created China Wide Web, which is the literal translation of 中国互联网 as first used by English editions of Xinhua News Agency and China Daily.

However, technically China Wide Web uses the same Internet and Intranet technology but with information predominantly being provided in Chinese language and with Chinese search engines also mainly serving Chinese language users. Not surprisingly neither Google nor Yahoo but locally developed search engines Baidu and Sohu dominate the searching market on the China wide web. Of course, China Wide Web is technically part of the World Wide Web thus, the term Internet though not its original phonetic translation of 因特网 but more meaningful translation of 互联网 is inter used and online users are often described as Netizens.

By the end of June 2009 the total number of Netizen in China reached 318 million hence making China the biggest online country in the world as confirmed by the graph below which was compiled by the New Media Trend Watch of the European Travel Commission [73]

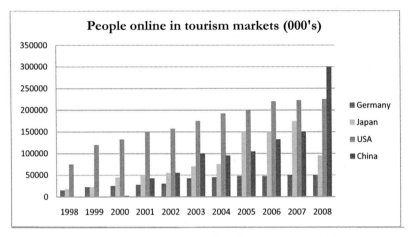

Fig. 3: Comparison of people online in four markets (000's)

Moreover, comparing to 350 TV channels in China there are over 2 million Chinese websites now which also dwarfs the number of publications of about 9,000 nationwide thus, the China Wide Web or Internet in China has become the primary media which reaches the largest number of users nationwide.

More importantly, it is an easily understand fact that most Netizens are well educated or being educated, who also have the financial resources to have computers and to subscribe online access, they are likely to be eager to find out more about outside world. Thus, they are the more likely target for tourism promotion organisations. It is very interesting to note that even a growing number of the older generation in China who makes up 13.5% of China's international travel market[74] are also finding the Internet to be the most convenient media for accessing destination information.

---

[73] ETC New Media Trend Watch: http://www.newmediatrendwatch.com.
[74] "Silver Marketing" in China International Business August 2009, p.19.

Moreover, it is a well known fact that there may be without exception every company in China that is serious about sending Chinese overseas would be heavily dependent on the internet for both information and communication as it is well known fact that Chinese travel professionals prefer using MSN or other instant messaging programs to communicate between each other and foreign partners for instant response. Therefore, it is only natural to conclude that destination promotion organisations need to make full use of online marketing to reach both the outbound travel trade as well as the millions of actual travellers throughout China and throughout year.

2.3 How best to use the China wide web to promote foreign destinations

2.3.1 Developing Chinese website

The first step is to translate your information into Chinese in a professional manner. They can then be integrated to Chinese web pages so as to be accessible directly and also easily found by users in China. It is important to realize that not only computers in China are loaded with Chinese operating systems but also the majority of Chinese people (even seasoned travellers), can only use or they prefer to use Chinese language. Moreover, the same written Chinese solves the problem of many different spoken dialects such as Cantonese because Chinese people of all parts of China understand the same written characters.

While translating and designing Chinese web pages are not most challenging. However, to do it professionally one needs to engage experienced local companies that understand the terminology of the travel trade in China and the technical and design team have to be skilled in designing the Chinese web pages that can be viewed by any known Chinese browsers. Those who sought the easiest solution of using some kind of automatic translation software to translate their own website into Chinese probably would not realized the negative impression that bad often completely mistranslation by any software can create especially when translating into a completely different language such as Chinese.

2.3.2 Online marketing in China

Those organizations who spent much money in translating and developing professional web pages that are merely embedded into their own

143

website that are not even hosted in China or without any attempt to index and meta-tag in Chinese search engines, would simply waste money because without reaching the potential users in China. However, a good Chinese website would not achieve its objective of attracting Chinese visitors. Therefore, the most important step once a Chinese website has been professionally created is to ensure that it is hosted in China or at least easily accessible and searchable by Chinese travel trade and travellers who are predominantly using local search engines in Chinese. It is also very important to keep in mind that "search engines will always show first sites in local languages".[75]

In the case of online marketing in China it is even preferred for Chinese web pages to be hosted in China not only for easy indexing and online marketing but also for easy accessing the site because the sheer number of 328 million Netizens can create big traffic jams that is far worse than traffic congestion often seen during rush hours in Beijing and Shanghai, which also due to large number of users. The bandwidth linking the China Wide Web and the World Wide Web could not cope with the large number and still fast growing number of Chinese Netizens getting online each day. Furthermore, it is also well known fact that Chinese authorities place restrictions and often bland ban on certain websites that are hosted overseas although mainly to prevent politically sensitive information and pornographic websites. However if your website is hosted by a common server which happens to host certain websites that Chinese authorities wish to block, then the server or certain bandwidth maybe affected altogether and thus, will prevent Chinese users to access your pure travel related information.

To host websites in China, one needs to engage professional companies again because Chinese authorities are yet to open the web hosting market to foreign entities. Until that happens the internet in China is very much controlled hence the real meaning of China wide web where each website, IP address and ICP i.e. internet content provider has to be registered with relevant authorities. Not surprisingly the main registration website of the Ministry of Industry and Information Technology i.e. http://www.miibeian.gov.cn recorded almost 300 million actual visitors by now. Due to the complexity of registration of registering Chinese web addresses and the necessity of hosting those in China foreign desti-

---

[75] http://www.newmediatrendwatch.com/world-overview/91-online-travel-market.

nation marketing organizations are advised to engage experienced local companies to do so.

2.3.3 Targeting the Outbound Travel Market

It is not even enough to simply pick any "good" online marketing company because not all online marketing companies specialize in the travel and tourism sector. As a matter of fact, engaging an experienced tourism marketing companies with expertise in online marketing and offline support is paramount important because such a company would have the means to reach the entire outbound travel trade and millions Chinese travellers.

2.4 Case Study — China Business Network

The pioneer in the field of marketing foreign destinations in China online is China Business Network which was the avant-garde in the internet development in China back in the middle of 1990s. Benefiting from the vast experience in business consultancy and targeted marketing services the China Business Network now provides destination marketing and PR representation for a large number of tourism promotion authorities and businesses in the travel and tourism sector across the world.

2.4.1 CBN Travel Service

With the outbound travel from China growing rapidly China Business Network established own travel services under the strong brand of CBN Travel Service. Over the years CBN Travel Service has been supporting many groups of senior government officials (including Ministers, Chairmen of CNTA and provincial Governors) and business executives as well as the high end of discerning Chinese visitors travelling overseas.

CBN Travel Service was proud to be chosen to provide the destination management services to the Beijing Olympic Torch Relay which was the best acknowledgement of the high quality services that CBN travel service has been providing to many other groups of VIPs as well as large event such as CCTV's best known program - "The Same Song" Concert with over 3000 audience singing and dancing live with Chinese stars.

2.4.2 Dedicated Outbound Travel Portal - World Travel Online

With such tangible experience of handling Chinese visitors China Business Network has the unique advantage to provide foreign tourism authorities and travel businesses with targeted marketing activities and promotional supports using specialized and the most prominent outbound travel portal called World Travel Online which had an unique web address http://lvyou168.cn in Chinese on the China Wide Web. "Lüyou" is the Chinese word for "travel", hence the English demo home page of the World Travel Online is www.travel168.net. The website provides comprehensive information in Chinese on: the latest Government regulations about going abroad, procedure of getting passport and the necessary visas, local custom and living conditions as well as recommended foreign destinations etc.

China Business Network also reaches the entire outbound travel trade by operating the China Travel and Tourism Club (CTTC) which is a non-profit membership based organization that provides up-to-date market intelligence and privileged services to over 26,000 travel and tourism related authorities and businesses and has over 18,000 professional members across China hence the China Travel and Tourism Club is often regarded as the equivalent to the Meridian Club for the World Travel Market.

2.3.4 Complete and value-added services for promoting foreign destinations in China
Destination promotion is certainly not achieved only online. As a matter of fact, China Business Network provides tourism promotion authorities and travel businesses with complete value-added services that include:

1. Functioning as GSA or PR Marketing Agent in China to promote foreign destinations during all the relevant international exhibitions from CITM to CIBTM, COTTM, from BITE, GITF to WTF that sought supports and certainly benefited from CBN's unmatched resources and complete coverage of the outbound travel from China. For professional presentation during any exhibitions the China Business Network would professionally design and print Chinese collaterals locally and more cost effectively in China that would be delivered to any exhibition, road show or workshop in China. When a destination decides to participates in any such event directly CBN would invite qualified travel trade professionals and senior outbound decision makers coming to meet with delegations of foreign destinations.

2. Organising destinations road shows or workshop and presentation seminars by qualifying and inviting travel trade professionals, selecting venue and negotiating best packages as well as providing full support during such events and following up interested contacts and even making sales calls to qualified Chinese tour operators and corporate travel organisers on behalf of represented destinations.

3. Providing continuous PR marketing support by releasing news and e-shots to travel trade as well as other media not only travel related items but also any positive news or action such as visit by government officials to and from the destination. Such news followed by destination information are very important in China because many Chinese are politically sensitive that follow the relationship between China and a destination on the political and economical fronts that in turn would raise their interest in visiting such a destination and even decide to invest in such destinations that China demonstrates to supports. CBN Travel service can actually provide practical supports for mutual visits of government officials and tourism professionals including Fam trips.

4. The above offline activities are necessary compliment to the cost effective online marketing activities that CBN provide as a complete package that begins with professionally translating, creatively implementing a comprehensive website or a number of web pages in Chinese and hosting them on our dedicated servers in China.

5. CBN also provides targeted direct email marketing (DEM) by sending e-short and news releases in Chinese directly to the decision-makers of all the corporate travel organizers and outbound tour operators that are members of China Travel and Tourism Club.

6. Assisting clients to embed the same Chinese presentation into own official website to save clients money from engaging any third party to simply translating a website into Chinese which would be lost in the Internet jungle without targeted marketing to the Chinese market.

7. Providing Chinese travel trade and travelling public with direct access to destination on the award winning outbound travel portal "World Travel Online" via clearly categorized destination and section headings.

8. Last but not least CBN provides comprehensive online marketing services by continuous indexing and meta-tagging key words related

to clients destinations in Chinese search engines and throughout the China Wide Web so that to make sure even those Chinese travel trade professionals or individual travellers who are merely searching for destination information will always bring up the relevant information in Chinese about the clients destination that will help them in making an informed decision of visiting that destination.

For providing such comprehensive and result generating activities China Business Network received numerous prestigious awards such as CTW Chinese Tourists Welcoming Award for overall performance i.e. for its comprehensive services to the outbound travel from China and also for supporting large number of tourism promotion authorities and commercial companies in the travel and tourism sector from all around the world.

The successful outbound travel portal developed by the China Business Network --- the World Travel Online was awarded "The Best Website for Outbound Travel from China".

Such high profile awards are the best testimony of CBN's unrivalled expertise in online marketing and tested experience in destination promotion off line as well as practical experience in handling large number of Chinese visitors. Not surprisingly China Business Network was also among the first three proud winners of the "China Outbound Tourism Quality Label".

Conclusion

By analyzing the sheer size of the fast growing Chinese outbound market and the unique difficulties that foreign destinations marketing organizations have been encountering as well as the media that most Chinese travel trade professionals and actual travellers use for finding destination information it is clear that the most cost effective way and indeed, in most cases as the first step of getting started with the Chinese market is to professionally designing and setting up a Chinese website that has to be hosted and marketed in China in the targeted way in order to reach its intended audience. Destination marketers need to understand the uniqueness of the China Wide Web in order to take full advantage of the online marketing potential to attract Chinese traveller.

Furthermore, such targeted online marketing activities need to be complemented by traditional offline supports such as attending exhibitions, organising road shows, PR events, Fam trips etc. that require the support of experienced tourism promotion and marketing company such as the China Business Network which has proven to be avant-garde in destination marketing and supporting tourism promotion authorities in promoting foreign destinations in China both online, offline from 360 degree integrated campaign to interactive 3D marketing that proven to be the most successful way of marketing foreign destinations in China.

References

China Internet Network Information Center (CNNIC)
   http://chinadigitaltimes.net/china/internet-growth.

ETC New Media Trend Watch: *The European Travel Commission*
   www.newmediatrendwatch.com.

ETC New Media Trend Watch
   http://www.newmediatrendwatch.com/world-overview/91-online-travel-market.

WIKI ANALYSIS: *Rise of China's Middle Class*
   http://www.wikinvest.com/concept/Rise_of_China's_Middle_Class.

Yang Xiyun (2009): *"Silver Marketing" in China International Business August 2009, p.19.*

Abbreviations

ADS	Approved Destination Status
AEF	Straits Exchange Foundation
ARATS	Association for Relations Across the Taiwan Straits
BITE	Beijing International Tourism Expo
BITTM	Beijing International Travel & Tourism Market
CARICOM	Caribbean Community
CBN	China Business Network
CCTV	China Central Television
CIBTM	China Incentive Business Travel & Meetings Exhibition
CIFIT	China International Fair for Investment and Trade
CITM	China International Travel Mart
CITS	China International Travel Services
CNNIC	China Internet Network Information Center
CNTA	China National Tourism Administration
CNTO	China National Tourist Office
COQ	China Outbound Tourism Quality Label
COTRI	China Outbound Tourism Research Institute
COTTM	China Outbound Travel and Tourism Market
CPTM	Consejo de Promoción Turística de Mexico (Mexican Council for the Promotion of Tourism)
CTEA	Cross-Strait Tourism Exchange Association
CTO	Caribbean Tourism Organisation
CTS	China Travel Service
CTTC	China Travel and Tourism Club
CTW	Chinese Tourists Welcoming Award
CYTS	China Youth Travel Service
DEM	Direct Email Marketing
DMC	Destination Management Companies
ETC	European Travel Commission
EU	European Union
FAM tours	Familiarization tours
FDI	Foreign Direct Investment
GDP	Gross Domestic Product
GITF	Guangzhou International Travel Fair
INM	Mexico's National Institute of Migration
JHTA	Jamaica Hotel & Tourist Association
JTB	Jamaica Tourist Board
MAKS	Marketing Cooperation Cities in Schleswig-Holstein
MICE	Meetings, Incentives, Conferencing, Exhibitions
MOT	Ministry of Tourism
MoU	Memorandum of Understanding
PPP	Purchasing Power Parity

PATA	Pacific Asia Travel Association
QITE	Qingdao International Tourism Expo
SAR	Special Administrative Region
TAAT	Travel Agent Association of Taiwan
TASH	Schleswig-Holstein Tourism Agency
UN	United Nation
UNCTAD	United Nations Conference on Trade and Development
UNESCO	United Nations Educational, Scientific and Cultural Organization
UNWTO	United Nations World Tourism Organization
USP	Unique Selling Proposition
UWI	University of the West Indies
VIP	Very Important Person
WEF	World Economic Forum
WTF	World Travel Fair

About the authors

MBA, Berenice Aceves *is General Manager of the COTRI China Outbound Tourism Research Institute in the West Coast University of Applied Sciences in Heide, Germany. She has studied both her Bachelor in International Relations and Master in Business Administration in Mexico. She is currently a Doctorate student in the Catholic University of Eichstätt-Ingolstadt in Germany with the dissertation topic: Imaginary geography in a collective society: the Chinese Outbound Tourism. She's been a visiting lecturer in different institutions with subjects as international tourism, management, interculturalism and languages. She has successfully organized and presented her research in the Workshop "Strategies to attract Chinese tourists to Mexico" last October 2008 in Mexico City. Previous COTRI, Berenice Aceves worked as an Economic Analyst in the Economical and Commercial Section of the Embassy of the People's Republic of China in Mexico and developed a Chinese Outbound tourism project in Beijing, China (2007-2008) supported by the Mexico City government.*

Prof. Dr. Wolfgang Georg Arlt FRGS (M.A. in Sinology and PhD in Political Sciences at FU Berlin), *is the founder and director of the COTRI China Outbound Tourism Research Institute, based in Heide/Holstein and Shanghai. He has been engaged in European-Chinese business and tourism relations for 35 years and visited the People's Republic of China more than 100 times, starting in 1978. His current academic position is professor for international tourism management at the West Coast University of Applied Sciences, Germany, being also a visiting professor at several Chinese and European universities and fellow of the Royal Geographical Society (UK), research fellow of the APC for Leisure Studies at Zhejiang University and former research fellow of the Japanese Society for the Promotion of Science. He has published widely on China's outbound tourism included the seminal Routlegde monograph «China's Outbound Tourism» (2006) and other publications in English, Chinese, and German. Prof. Dr. Arlt is co-editors of the series «Schriftenreihe des Instituts für Management und Tourismus».*

Diploma-Geographer Rainer Fugmann, *born in 1982, studied Geography of Leisure and Tourism at the Catholic University of Eichstätt-Ingolstadt (Germany) and at the University Iberoamericana Puebla (Mexico). His diploma-thesis about the Chinese Outbound-Tourism won the DGT Science Award at the ITB 2009 in the category 'best paper in terms of industry relevance'. Currently he is a PhD candidate at the Catholic University of Eichstätt-Ingolstadt, working on a project on the Chinese Inbound Tourism to Germany.*

M.A., Gerlis Fugmann, *born in 1979, studied Geography, Anthropology and Archaeology at the Rheinische Friedrich-Wilhelms University Bonn (Germany) and at the University of Northern British Columbia (Canada). Her magister thesis with the title "Economic development perspectives in the state-building process of Nunavut" explored current development in mining and tourism in this Arctic territory. Currently she is working as a research associate at the Department of Geography of the Justus Liebig University Giessen while completing a*

PhD project focusing on a regional comparison of development perspectives for Inuit regions in the Circumpolar North. Her PhD project was partially funded by a fellowship of the DAAD.

Prof. Dr. Ching Lin Pang, *Lecturer and senior staff at the research unit IMMRC (Interculturalism, Migration and Minorities Research Centre) of Social Sciences at the Catholic University Leuven; Lecturer Intercultural Management and Chinese culture and language at HEC-Ecole de Gestion in University of Liège. Her research topics are anthropology of ethnicity, interculturalism and migration including migration and diversity policies and programs, super diversity, gender issues linked to migration, immigrant entrepreneurship and ethnic precincts, diaspora formations/transnationalism, second generation Chinese, return migration (policies) with a geographical focus on Asia (China, Japan and India).*

Dr. Taleb Rifai, *current Secretary General for the United Nations World Tourism Organization (UNWTO), officially elected in October 2009. Since 2006 he was appointed for Deputy Secretary-General of UNWTO and before as Assistant Director-General of the International Labour Organization (ILO) during 2003-2006. Prior to this appointment, he served in several ministerial portfolios in the government of Jordan as Minister of Tourism and Antiquities, Minister of Information and Minister of Planning and International Cooperation. Dr. Rifai was also actively involved in policy making and developing investment strategies in his capacity as Director General of the Investment Promotion Corporation (IPC) in Jordan (1995-1997). Moreover he headed Jordan's first Economic Mission to Washington DC, promoting trade, investments, and economic relations between Jordan and the USA (1993-1995). Dr. Rifai received education in Architectural Engineering from the University of Cairo, same major for Master in Chicago/USA and PhD in Urban Design and Regional Planning in Philadelphia/USA. He began his career as Professor of Architecture, Planning and Urban Design at the University of Jordan during 1973-1993.*

David L. Shields, *deputy director of tourism-marketing at the Jamaica Tourist Board since January, 2004. Known for his solid track record in designing and implementing creative marketing campaigns for the Caribbean region, Mr. Shields is responsible for marketing Jamaica's tourism product at a global level. Previously, Shields served as director of market development with Air Jamaica Vacations, based in Florida, where he designed powerful communications plans and initiated the analysis of demographic and psychographic profiles of consumers in major U.S.-Caribbean He is a graduate of the University of the West Indies with a Bachelor of Science (Hons.) degree in management studies and a Master of Science degree in accounting. He also holds a diploma in restaurant management from the Colonel Sanders Technical Institute in Kentucky and another in travel and tourism marketing awarded by Henry Stewart Conference Studies in London. He has completed courses in planning, creating and managing Web sites at the University of Toronto, and at the Global Knowledge Training Center in Santa Clara, CA. gateways.*

Dr. Adam Wu *is the Chief Operating Officer of the China Business Network whose slogan "brings the world to China and takes Chinese to the world" which summarizes the activities of CBN. As part of the China Business Network, CBN Travel Service supports Chinese official delegations, business groups visiting other parts of the worlds, also undertakes special events that often catch the attention of the world such as Olympic Torch Relay, World Expo 2010 promotion etc. Leading an experienced team Adam has been directly involved in advising many foreign tourism authorities and travel businesses with targeted marketing activities and promotional supports in China. He has also been invited to speak during various travel exhibitions, conferences and marketing summit as well as being interviewed by news media both online and offline. Expanding on his early experience with successful Internet projects including Chinapages.com, the first ever web site in China initiated by Jack Ma who later developed Alibaba.com, Adam was the initiator and co-founder of the World Travel Online in Chinese i.e. http://lvyou168.cn which is dedicated to outbound travel from China and has been awarded "The Best Website for Outbound Travel from China" and also won the prestigious CTW Golden Award.*

Prof. Zhang Guangrui *is the Director of Tourism Research Centre of Chinese Academy of Social Sciences (CASS TRC), Beijing, The CASSTRC is the only institution of tourism studies in the Chinese Academy of Social Sciences sponsored by the central government. It is a member of China National Tourism Association at home and a member ATLAS ASIA abroad. Professor Zhang is one of the earliest and active tourism researchers in the Academy. In the past decade or so, he has published a few books, over hundred academic papers, and participated and chaired a dozen of major projects sponsored by the national and CASS grants and made many field study and policy recommendation reports to the central and local governments. He has provided consulting service for local governments in tourism planning. Since 2000, Prof. Zhang has been the editor-in-chief of the annual Green Book of China's Tourism entitled China's Tourism Development: Analysis & Forecast. His major interests of studies include international tourism policies, tourism planning and development.*

M.A., Zhang Yang, *After finishing her studies in tourism management at the Sichuan University of China, she is now a Ph.D student in History and Culture College of Sichuan University. From September of 2008 until now, she has been promoted by the China Scholarship Council and studying Interculturalism, Migration and Minority Research Center of Catholic University of Leuven as a joint-promotion Ph. D student. Her research topics are the conservation and tourism exploitation of culture heritage, relationship, contact and communication between host society and tourists.*

中 国 出 境 游 研 究 所

COTRI China Outbound Tourism Research Institute

COTRI is the world's leading independent research institute for analysis, consulting and quality assessment relating to the Chinese Outbound Tourism market.

The China Outbound Tourism Research Institute offers information, analysis, publications, consulting, advice and coaching for destinations and companies interested in the biggest Asian source market in international tourism – China. COTRI is based in Heide/Germany (headquarter) and in Shanghai/China.

COTRI provides current and background information about Chinese Outbound tourism on its websites www.china-outbound.com, its Premium Content website www.win-chinese-tourists.com and in www.chinatraveltrends.com, the authoritative one-stop resource portal and travel industry community on China outbound tourism.

COTRI organizes workshops both public and in-house. COTRI customized workshops have been taking place in Europe, Asia, Central America, the Caribbean and South America. COTRI verifies companies and institutions engaged in providing excellent services for Chinese visitors awarding the COQ China Outbound Tourism Quality Label.

COTRI is closely working together with the UNWTO, PATA, China Tourist Academy (CTA), the Tourism Research Institute of the Chinese Academy for Social Sciences and other international organizations, national and regional tourism boards, private companies, universities and experts from many countries.

Current COTRI publications

- COTRI/PATA: *Are you ready? For Chinese International Travellers.*
  Self-learning programme for tourism managers and professionals to prepare for the Chinese Outbound Tourism source market.
- CTA/COTRI: *Annual Report of China Outbound Tourism Development 2009/2010.*
  The survey is edited by the CTA China Tourist Academy, a dedicated research institute of the National Tourism Administration of the People's Republic of China (CNTA). The English version is published in cooperation with COTRI.

For more information, please visit www.china-outbound.com.